Hanrahan + Meyers Architects

The Four States of Architecture

ACKNOWLEDGEMENTS

We would like to thank the following individuals who have worked for us over the years. Their efforts have made an enormous contribution to the work shown in this book.

Scott Enge

Matthew Baird

James Slade

Guy Maxwell

Jane Wason

John Flynn

Claire Lyster

Martha Coleman

Betsy Davis

Stephan de Bever

Kevin Lee

Dukho Yeon

Jason Holmes

Dan Cheung

Lisa Hsiao

Christopher Chew

Brian Corbett

Phillip Binkert

Brooks Dunn

Joseph Kosinski

Curtis Augspurger

Eric Cobb

David Teeple

Special thanks to:

Rhett Russo

Lawrence Zeroth

Sam Leung

Corvin Matei

PHOTOGRAPHY CREDITS

Peter Aaron, © Esto Photographics
Singer Residence: pp 26 (below), 27, 28 (below), 30, 31, 32-3; Schrom Studios: pp 46, 47, 48, 50, 51, 52, 53, 54-5; Arts International: pp 56-57, 58, 59 (above), 60, 61, 62-63; Loft Residence: pp 66, 67, 69, 71, 72, 73, 74, 75; Hunts Point Performance Center: pp 102 (below), 103, 104 (above), 105 (above), 107, 109, 110-1.

Jack Pottle, © Esto Photographics
Interpretive Center model: pp 13 (above), 14, 15, 16-17; Hudson River House model: pp 19, 24-5, Sagaponak House model: pp 77, 83; Hunts Point model: pp 106, 108 (below), Women's Museum model: p 113; Latimer Gardens model: p 127.

Eduard Hueber
Red Hook Center for the Arts: pp 37, 40 (above), 41 (above), 42, 44-5; Alves House: pp 117, 118 (both above), 120-1.

Rhett Russo
Singer Residence model: p 29; Alves House model: p 119 (above).

Lily Wang
Waterline, Canal Street model: pp 87 (left column), 89 (above), 90 (top and below left).

James Comer
Windmills. Tehachapi, California, p 64: reproduced with permission from *Taking Measures - Across the American Landscape* p 85; James Corner, Alex S Maclean: Yale University Press, 1996.

Cover: Michael Schrom and Company Studios, Long Island City, New York
Page 4: Singer Residence, East Hampton, New York

First published in Great Britain in 2002 by
WILEY-ACADEMY

A division of
JOHN WILEY & SONS
Baffins Lane
Chichester
West Sussex PO19 1UD

ISBN: 0-471-49652-9

Other Wiley Editorial Offices
New York • Weinheim • Brisbane • Singapore • Toronto

Design Liz Brown

Printed and bound in Italy

Hanrahan + Meyers Architects

The Four States of Architecture

contents

forewords

The work of Thomas Hanrahan and Victoria Meyers represents an exemplary reformulation of the modern in a post-modern world. A full generation after the collapse of late International Style, Hanrahan + Meyers' architecture demonstrates that the response to the banalities of that time was never limited to the arid historicism that dominated until the 1990s.

The four themes that loosely organise the work presented here are for the most part familiar in the larger lexicon of modern architecture. However, the work demonstrates the fertility of these concepts, reformulated in terms of contemporary discourse. Fittingly, the first of the four themes is the horizon, the unreachable attraction of the modern spirit that not only disappears each day but is reconstituted the next.

For the past two centuries, architecture has both grown and been diminished by the advent of an increasingly mediated world. For instance, the role of architecture as a principal source of information has been greatly challenged. Other aspects have been recast. Vitruvius could never have imagined that one of the 'delights' of architecture might be its increasingly potent role as a touchstone of the real in a highly simulated world. The work of Hanrahan + Meyers demonstrates an instinctive grasp of contemporary architecture's potential for framing real experience, rather than searching for the means to fold architecture into a larger media environment, one to which it can only contribute marginally.

Terence Riley
Chief Curator, Architecture and Design, Museum of Modern Art, New York

The career of Thomas Hanrahan and Victoria Meyers follows the path of young New York City architects; beginning with interior projects – loft renovations and studio spaces, competitions, houses and more recently, public buildings. With every project they have pursued both meaning and physicality. They walk the path between theory and built work, holding both as important guidelines – touching each side, but always keeping balance.

Their work possesses the quality of cool thoughtfulness. One sees the intelligence that directs their search. Clarity and order are so difficult to achieve. And once achieved, it is so easy to overlook these qualities. So it is important to call attention to the lucidity that gives authority to all of their work. Rigour is a quiet struggle. Hanrahan + Meyers engage in the struggle, they win, and then they sing.

Billie Tsien
Tod Williams Billie Tsien & Associates, New York

introduction

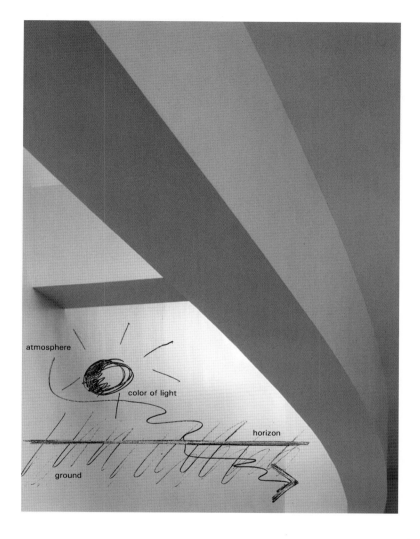

'The Four States of Architecture' is a reinterpretation of the classical understanding of matter and the physical world. In this world the four states consisted of earth, air, fire and water.

The four states of architecture in this book rename that body of knowledge. In the work of Hanrahan + Meyers these states become ground, atmospheres, the colour of light, and horizon. This renaming of the basic ways of understanding the world is an attempt to personalise the common elements of everyday life and make them an artistic narrative for a body of work.

Within this depiction, not only are these four states understood as radically active and different from their classical counterparts, but it is also understood that architecture can fully embody these states, that is architecture as line, as light, as non-mass, as the ground itself.

This book presents 14 projects, divided into four sections, each named for one of the four states of architecture: ground, atmospheres, colour of light, and horizon. Each project in each section presents a unique interpretation of that physical construct of the world, and becomes an embodiment of certain characteristics of that condition. It is this body of work's relationship to the very essence of these states of architecture and to new and contemporary ideas about nature and the natural world that defines the work presented here, of Victoria Meyers and Thomas Hanrahan.

Victoria Meyers and **Thomas Hanrahan**

It is interesting to ponder the relationship between the wind, the horizon line and the car. Somehow each has the ability to refer back to the other.

The car's steel, glass and electronic circuitry have the means of referring back to the naturally occurring situations of the horizon and the wind. It moves constantly towards the horizon line. It is a machine in a perpetual state of striving to reach an unreachable and untouchable place.

The horizon is also an 'event' plane: a *tabula rasa* or universally acknowledged place of infinite stasis, with events happening above and below. The line itself, however, like all mathematical constructs, is pure idea. It is untouchable, except in our imaginations. Its reality is central to much of what makes our world. It itself, however, is an untouchable place.

As a line the horizon presents us with the dilemma of understanding the unknowable properties of a Euclidean mathematical construct: something that has substance as a thought but not as a real or tangible thing. The horizon confronts us on a daily basis. It is a space of 'infinity'. It is the subject of photography and art. It is a primary means of orientation in the world. And yet, it is also untouchable and unknowable. To touch the horizon is as ambiguous and unachievable as finding the end of a rainbow.

This unknowable construct forms the very basis of human understanding and orientation in the world. It is something we accept as 'given', as a means of orienting ourselves.

In art, when something is drawn parallel to the horizon it indicates stasis or death. The most simple of iconographic symbols, a line drawn in the horizontal position indicates death; in the vertical, it symbolises life.

Wind likewise has its own history of intangibility. Wind is tied to relativity. Wind is blowing either because we are moving or because there is a change in pressure that causes air to move relative to us. Wind is relative.

Wind is also, in the absence of particles it carries along with it, invisible. In its invisibility it aligns itself with its brother horizon. Invisible things are difficult for us to know. We can measure wind, we can feel it, but we cannot see it. It is the very air we breathe and thus, like the horizon line, forms one of our basic ways of understanding who and how we are in the world.

For the most part, breath is unconscious for all of us. Yet it defines life itself. Without breath, we would cease to exist as living entities. Water and air are two of the basic parts of our being.

With the sound of the car the magic and the intangibility of the horizon and the wind are broken. The car is our iron horse: it is how we have reshaped our landscape to compensate for our bodies' inability to move across the land as quickly as we would like. Speed gives us access to the possession of an intangible landscape.

We are able to possess landscape by traversing it. By touching each part of the land we take possession of it.

In Africa there is a tribe that practises scarification by carving lines on the face of the participant. In this particular tribe, lines on the human body or in the earth signify the presence of human culture. Lines are an indication of civilisation. Lines on the face in this particular tribe are a means of telling the world, 'I am civilised. I have lines on my face' (Catherine Ingraham: *Architecture and the Burdens of Linearity*, pp.1–2, 'Dividing the land').

Cars are steel, glass and electronic circuitry at the whim of human pleasure. Roads and highways have become the American indication of civilisation. Come across a landscape in the USA without lines of roadways, and you will feel a sense of being in the wild: of being outside the reach of civilisation.

Cars bring us in direct contact with wind and the horizon. In the modern world it is as relevant to consider how a work of architecture will be read from the vantage of the car as it is to consider its image from a stationary point of view.

There was a school of architecture in Italy – the so-called Futurists – that designed architecture from the point of view of the traveller in the car. Los Angeles, which is a car culture, also designs buildings in relationship to the car more than the body of the person.

What is of interest in this discussion is how, as human beings, we experience profoundly moving and memorable moments in life. Many of our most important memories in the contemporary world are directly linked to the effects of all three experiences: wind, horizon, and car.

There is something levelling about that first moment of arriving at the ocean and taking in the view – of overlooking the endless edge where the plane of the water meets the sky: the line between water and air. As a moment of adolescent passage, learning to drive a car is something shared by all American teens. Nights when the wind howls join together in our imaginations, and put us into a state of mind to seek and appreciate shelter.

The car is a ubiquitous invention that has altered the appearance of the human landscape. From outer space the lines on the earth from the presence of so many cars are readable. Cars carve the earth as steadily and as forcefully as the wind.

Lines in the hand are a means of interpreting a life. The same sort of predictability is possible with the lines of highways viewed from outer space. The future is visible within and through the reading of lines. In many ways, the highway becomes the American restatement of the horizon line.

Victoria Meyers

opposite **two skies together: restating the horizon line**

Interpretive Center

Elise Chapin Wildlife Sanctuary. Chattanooga, Tennessee

1988

The Elise Chapin Wildlife Sanctuary Interpretive Center is a nature museum situated at the entrance to a natural sanctuary outside Chattanooga, Tennessee. It is intended as a public education and meeting facility, and the project design was the winning entry in a national competition.

The building was designed as an 'active instrument' for the study of natural and historical aspects of the sanctuary site. Primarily a single volume, the Interpretive Center projects into an existing natural 'bowl' in the landscape and is transformed by a number of spatial and technological interventions within its boundaries. These interventions are 'instruments' themselves, measuring air, water and wildlife, suggesting that technology can supplement our understanding of the natural world.

The programme for the Interpretive Center includes two galleries for the display of Native American and natural artifacts. One gallery will house a permanent collection, and a second gallery is for travelling exhibits. The programme also includes a kitchen, a meeting room for members of the Chattanooga Audubon Society, and an outdoor deck.

The entrance to the building is a large lobby. This space houses maps and a scale model of the sanctuary, and is a general orientation space for visitors. The lobby is designed to function even if the rest of the building is closed. The roof of the lobby participates as an important part of the Nature Interpretive Center: it is a large skylight which also operates as a solar panel.

The building has a wood and steel structure, and is sheathed in wood ship-lapped siding. Various inserted elements of the building are made of steel, aluminium and glass.

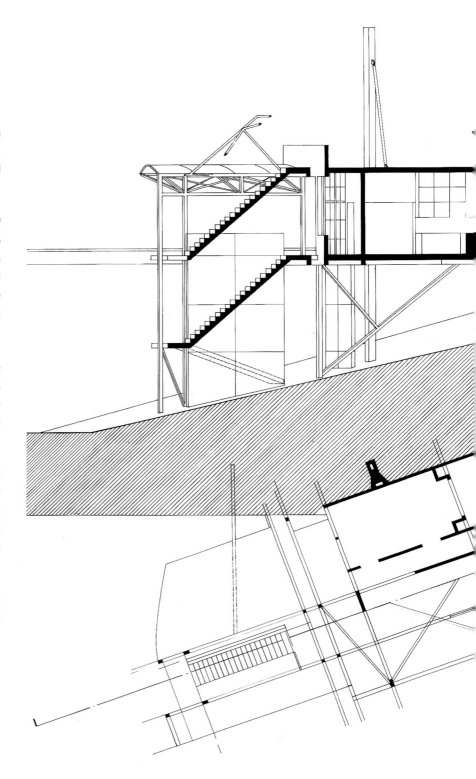

longitudinal section with plan

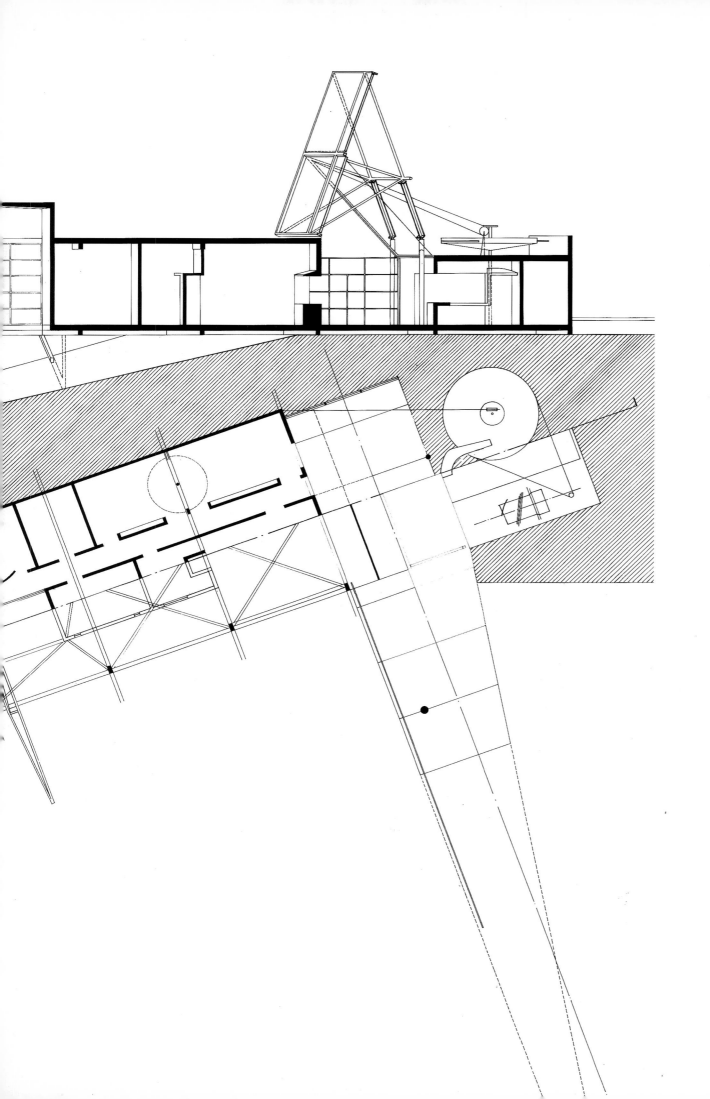

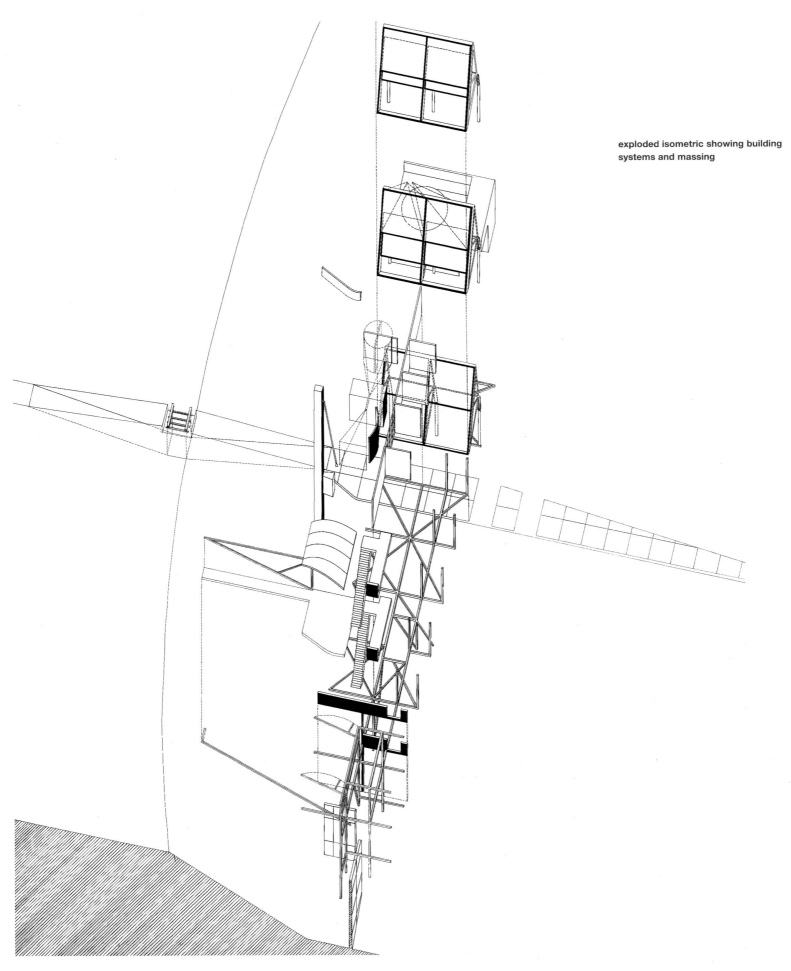

exploded isometric showing building
systems and massing

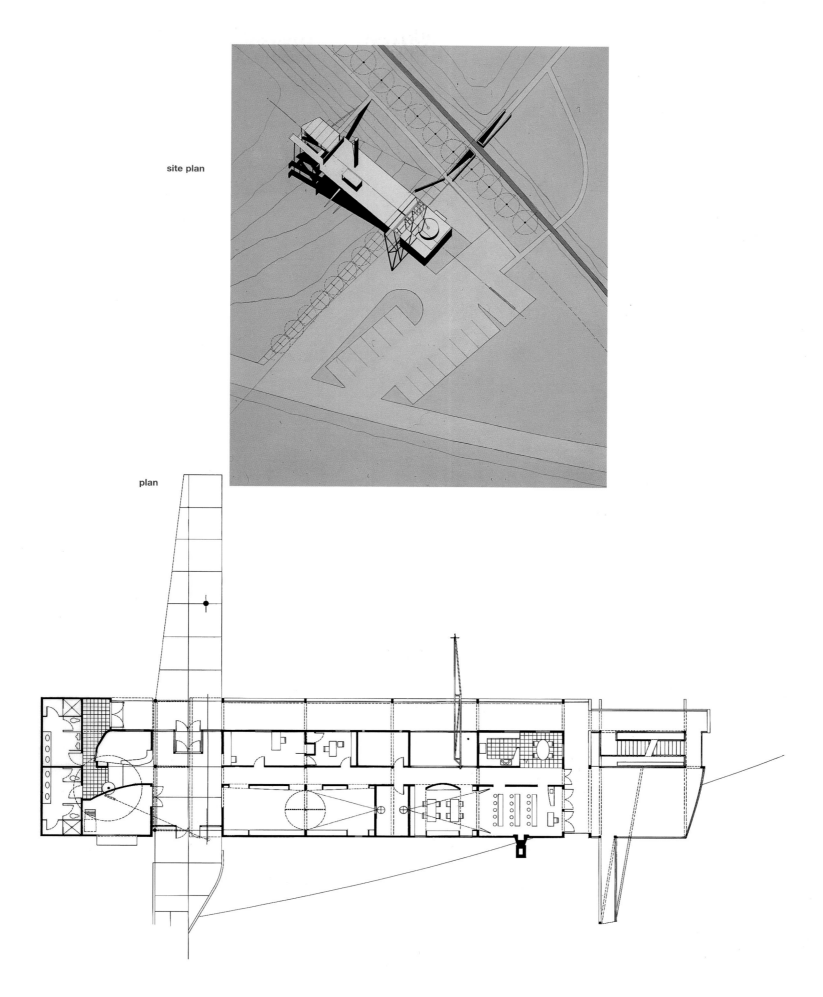

site plan

plan

13

opposite **model view looking northwest**

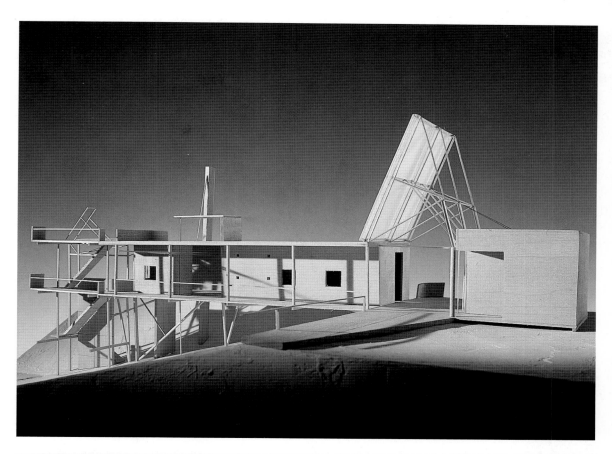

model view looking southwest, towards entry

model view looking towards outdoor deck

next page **perspective view of building as 'probe into nature'**

Hudson River House

Nyack, New York

1988

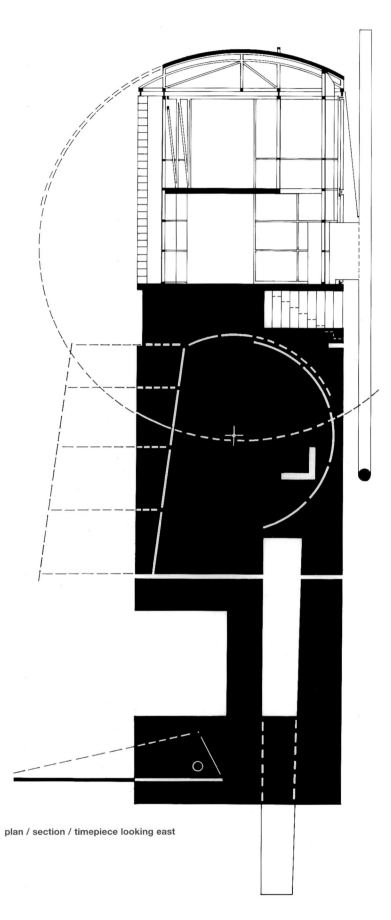

plan / section / timepiece looking east

Joseph Beuys inscribed new script on old script in a piece entitled *Clan* in 1964. The act of inscription yields a third text or meaning, a drawn Tower of Babel, and an unfinished work. This condition of superposition suggests new possibilities for architecture: the incorporation of multiple spatial ideas and technological systems within a single work, and an architecture literally animated by inhabitation.

This proposal is for a house in Nyack, New York. The site is a thin, steeply sloping parcel of land with approximately 55 feet of frontage onto the Hudson River. The overall size of the house is 2500 square feet.

The most dramatic feature of the site is its steep slope which gives approaching visitors a dramatic view of the Hudson River. The house is designed so that it would not be intrusive to that initial river view.

The site is carved into a series of impressions as one steps down the hillside. A post and beam system of wood, steel and aluminium completes spaces initiated by these original impressions. Glass and Kalwall panels form a third system: a 'kinetic superstructure' of movable parts that transform each space over time. A drawing entitled 'hieroglyphic graphic' depicts how the house was designed as a series of inscriptions written onto and into the site.

These kinetic structures allow spaces inside the house to change with time. The roof over the living area and master bedroom can be opened for ventilation or for viewing the sky. This is the 'timepiece' for the house. A semicircular curved wall frames a principal view from the living room and master bedroom towards the garden when it is in a 'closed position'; open, it frames the view towards the river. At the upper level a terrace is a slot of space which cuts through the house from north to south. A window at the southern edge of this slot has a movable sun screen which allows the view to be open or closed.

The materials proposed for the building are concrete masonry for the carved areas, and wood post and beam construction with steel fastening details for the framed construction. The curved wall of the living room is planned to be Kalwall. The roof is to be sheathed in anodised clear aluminium, with cut-out areas roofed with transparent glass skylights.

model view looking west,
towards living room wall

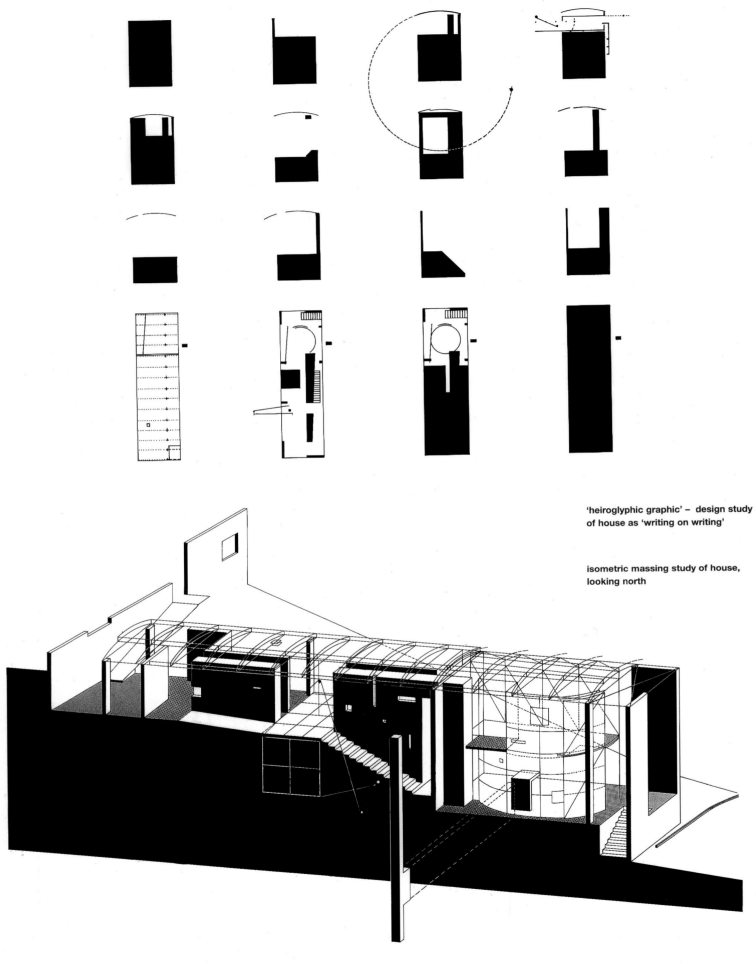

'heiroglyphic graphic' – design study
of house as 'writing on writing'

isometric massing study of house,
looking north

collage plan study for house

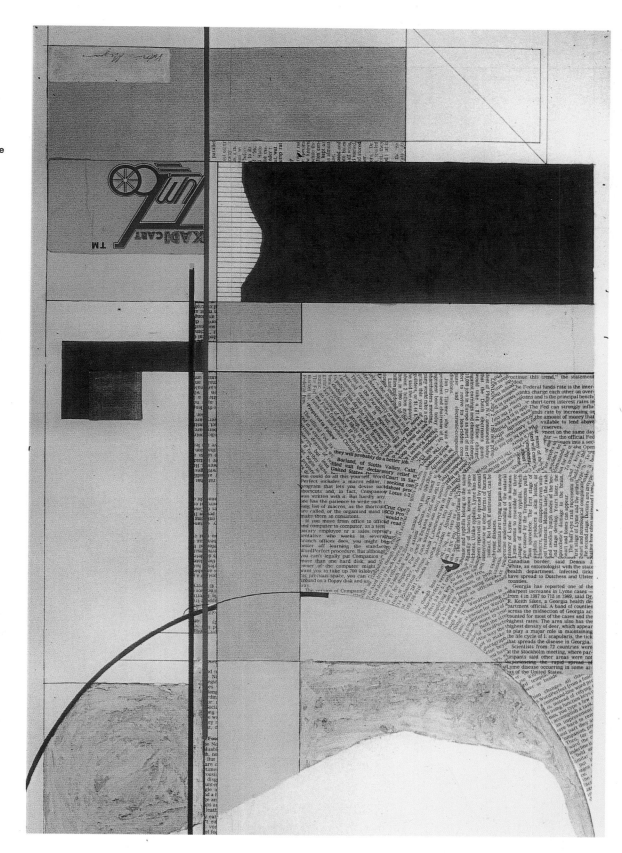

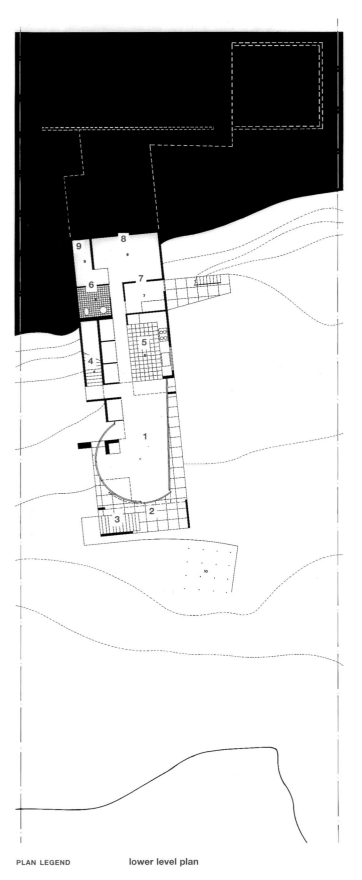

PLAN LEGEND

lower level plan

1. living
2. terrace
3. stair to lawn
4. stair to upper level
5. kitchen
6. bathroom
7. utility room
8. storage
9. mechanical

upper level plan

1. drive way
2. garage
3. stair down to
   entrance porch
4. entrance porch
5. entrance
6. corridor
7. guest bedroom
8. balcony
9. guest bath
10. master bath
11. open to below
12. stair down
13. master bedroom

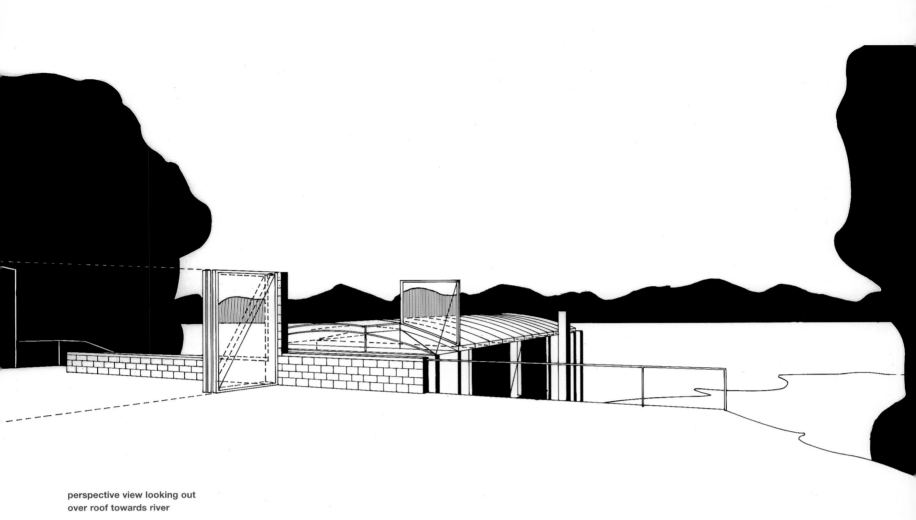

**perspective view looking out
over roof towards river**

next page **model view looking south**

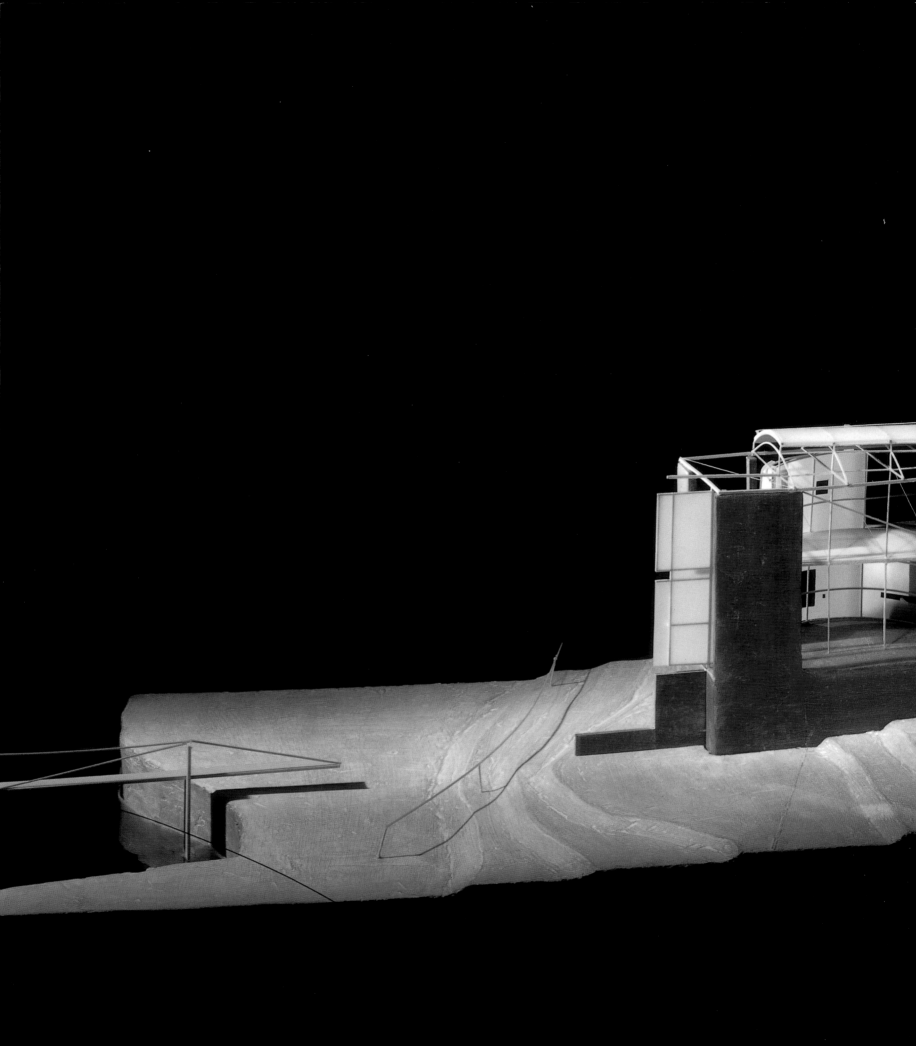

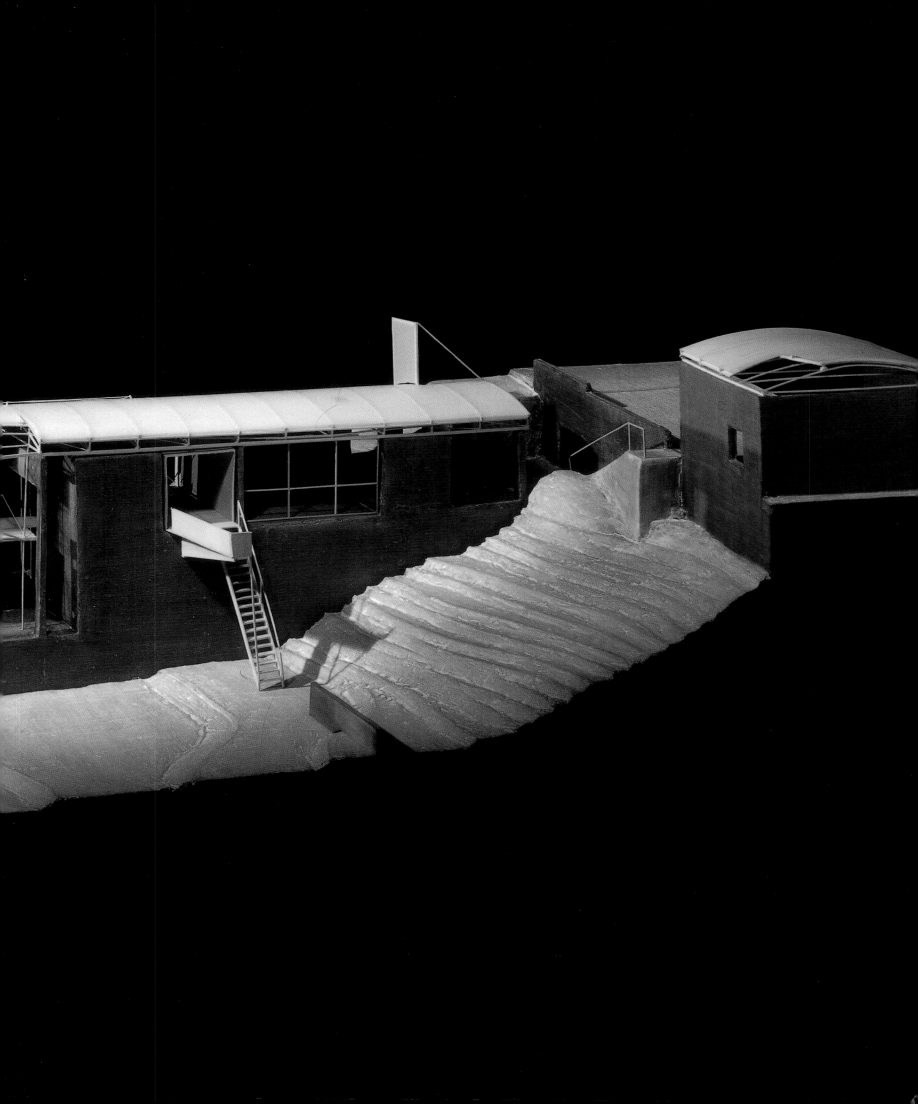

Singer Residence

East Hampton, New York

2001

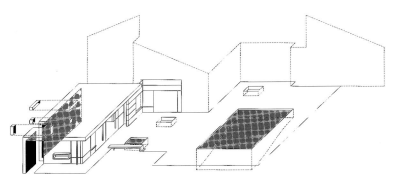

isometric view of pool house and pools

This project is a 1200-square-foot pool house in East Hampton, New York. The existing 2400-square-foot house is also renovated. The pool house is designed as a long, low, freestanding pavilion, with cedar siding stained a natural wood finish. It is meant to read as landscape, with the pool house becoming a shaped edge to the cedar deck that folds up into it. Copper cladding wraps the wall of a corridor connecting the pool house and the existing house.

The back wall of the pool house is freestanding and painted a brilliant, deep blue. This is a reference to the horizon line, bringing an artificial sky down to the ground and restating the line of the horizon within the new pool house. It reinforces the impression of the pavilion as a piece of 'artificial landscape'. The wall also refers to Luis Barragan's blue wall at Las Arboledas in Mexico City.

The blue of the pool and the soaking tub that sit in front of the pool house maintain a conversation with the blue horizon wall of the pavilion. Water and sky, and the beauty of cedar and copper combine to create a new, artificially constructed landscape.

Barragan: Plaza y Fuente del Bebedero

looking west, horizon line to left of pool house

plan

N

0 5

rock garden connection,
looking south

model showing pool house with pools
in foreground

model view toward 'horizon line'

opposite **detail view of west elevation, looking south towards pools**

master bath

master bedroom

next page **south elevation, looking towards new 'horizon line'**

colour of light

The work in this section is comprised of projects that focus on light. Light acts as both an organisational and an inspirational element.

Our clients, who have been mostly from the arts, respond to light. Light is a necessary condition for making art. It is also an instrument for creating theatre, and a place within a building that becomes a focus. Light enters at the place where there is an aperture between two conditions, inside and outside. Skylights, windows and doors are all means of giving the building a place for this intersection between nature – in the form of sunlight – and interior space to happen. Light is comprised of many colours and as the speed of light is slowed, through a prism or rain drop, for example, colours emerge.

There are places where architecture could be said to experience its most climactic moments. These are the very places in the project where those who inhabit them are drawn and where the space becomes most focused: 'towards the light'.

Victoria Meyers

opposite **a 'window' from Marfa, Texas**

Red Hook Center for the Arts

Brooklyn, New York

1999

Red Hook Center for the Arts examines the colour of light. Light is a palpable element within the language of the building.

Red Hook Center is a public art gallery, performance space and art education centre in Brooklyn. The building uses light to cut lines through a site located at an edge of the city, between Red Hook and the rest of Brooklyn.

The façade is a limestone frame with glass infill. The glass curtain wall floats within the freestanding limestone wall which frames a public art gallery where local artists show their work. A rectangular punch in this wall with a red frame and sandblasted glass blurs the proscenium between the street and the gallery. The blur, or soft focus, of this part of the façade becomes one of several moments of 'floating' proscenia within the building.

In the gallery a skylight cuts a 'line of light', marking the threshold between the gallery and an existing building it annexes. This line of light brings daylight into the gallery. A curving wall at the juncture between new and renovated space is painted bright red on its inside face. The red of this inner surface reflects back onto the white gallery wall, creating an area of reflected light.

Adjacent to the gallery is a theatre. This space has a deep blue proscenium that opens inwards, as well as out towards a landscaped area. The stage accommodates indoor and outdoor performances.

The lower level of the Red Hook Center houses a high school for the arts. There is a dance studio, art classrooms, a library and a computer graphics lab.

'Lines of light' make a place for theatre, performance, art, art education and dance in Red Hook. Light permeates the building. Broken into its colour spectrum light glows in hues of red, yellow and blue on different surfaces, marking edges between functions in the building.

site plan showing Brooklyn and Manhattan

opposite **view looking west towards building entrance**

36

isometric sketch study for building
massing

right **plan of building, including site**

far right **'lines of light': plan diagram
of how building activates through light**

SITE PLAN

1. public plaza
2. walkway: west 9th street to
   red hook houses
3. entrance pavillion/gallery
4. theater/multi-purpose
5. indoor/outdoor stage
6. outdoor theater seating
7. outdoor basketball court
8. playground
9. existing day care center
10. red hook houses

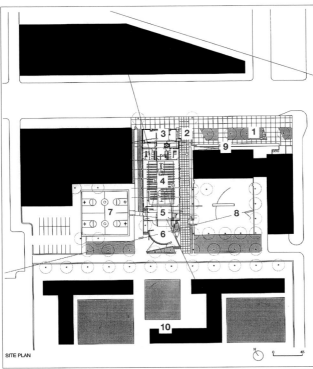

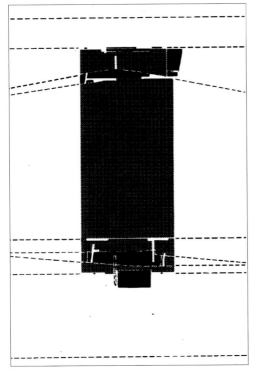

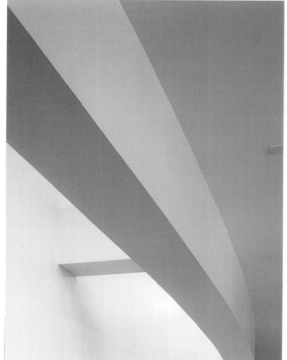

above **perspective study of building entrance elevation**

far left **skylight: the second 'line of light'**

left **watercolour perspective light study**

framing red: gallery wall

perspective massing study for building

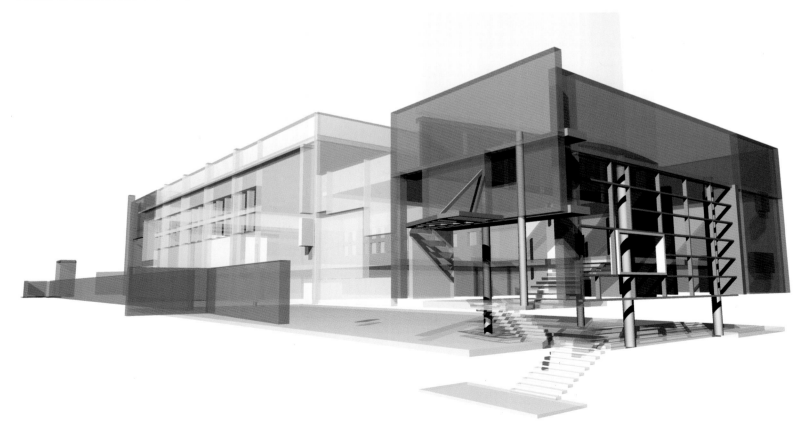

framing blue (sky): stage elevation

bird's-eye perspective: massing study

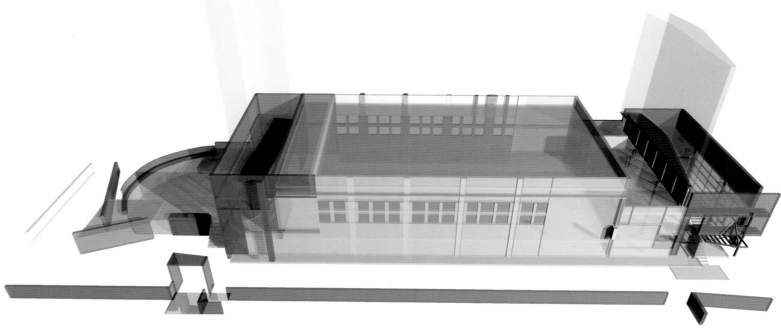

41

perspective study: line of light
between gallery and theatre

right **light wall**

far right **window above
entrance elevation**

next page **main elevation looking
towards gallery entrance pavilion**

below **in the gallery, looking towards
the red wall**

Michael Schrom and Company Studios

Long Island City, New York

2001

This project is a television studio comprising two primary areas: a public gallery and a stage. These are connected by a five-foot-thick 'light monitor' wall that runs the length of the studio.

The gallery is an open area with objects that float within it. A glass-enclosed conference room has an articulated ceiling with a large light monitor that reaches towards a roof skylight above. Tinted glass in the skylight colours the interior of the conference room monitor yellow. A freestanding maple stair sits in front of the conference room, describing a De Chiricoesque sequence from the gallery to a second-floor mezzanine. An open metal bridge connects the solid maple stair to the mezzanine.

The stage for filming is visible through a 15-foot-tall movable wall of steel and glass. The stage and galleria can be closed off from one another by a full-height curtain of green leather.

The studio's environment is animated by light and creative energy. The conference room's yellow skylight is underlined by a row of off-the-shelf florescent tube lights attached to the surface of the monitor. The freestanding maple stair is framed overhead by a skylight that is tinted blue. The 'light monitor' wall that runs the length of the studio has a series of openings cut into it, each rendering a different colour of light: red, blue, yellow, green and white. This was seen as a musical composition, which yields a changing volume of light and colour as one moves north to south.

The final design retains and celebrates the qualities of natural light that permeate the space. This celebration of light reinforces the work that takes place in the studio: the creation of films, which are themselves animations through light.

elevation looking towards 'light monitor' wall

opposite **looking towards entrance, with light pavilion to right**

46

view from entrance looking towards bridge, light pavilion to left

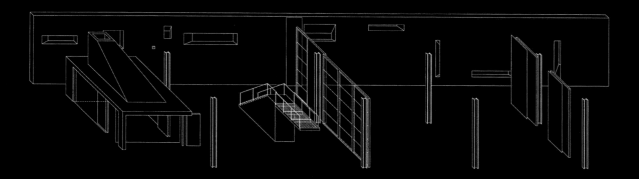

isometric massing study

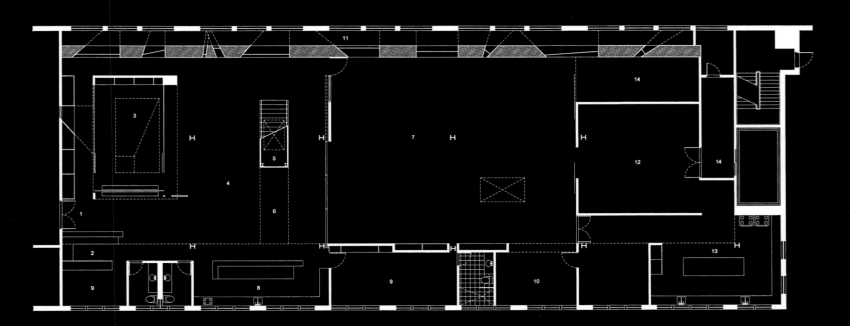

plan

light pavilion – under construction

looking towards light pavilion and
stair with glass and steel wall
separating gallery and studio

opposite **skylight over light
pavilion: yellow light**

opposite **looking through steel frame towards free-standing stair in main gallery**

stair portrait

bridge looking towards 'light pavilion'

next pages **looking towards mezzanine: view of Manhattan skyline**

Arts International Headquarters

New York

1999

Arts International is a contemporary arts organisation dedicated to the development and support of global exchanges in the arts. The headquarters building includes a 6000-square-foot gallery and performance space where artists can gather and show their work.

The gallery and performance space at Arts International is suffused with colour and light, borrowing light from perimeter windows. A red plaster wall beyond the gallery throws a red glow into the gallery from one corner. At the opposite corner a blue wall faces the gallery and casts a blue glow. The combination of colours, light and materials gives the space a sense of energy.

A series of interactive walls is also proposed. The central gallery with its stage that doubles as a conference area, research library and workroom is defined by an edge comprised of interactive surfaces. These surfaces are for installations of art, or video and other media in the gallery.

The stage is minimally delineated by a 20-foot-long by 1-foot-thick maple wall which supports a floating white plane above. The maple wall is covered by a grid of 30-inch by 30-inch by 16-inch-deep steel boxes.

Each end of the stage has clear glass walls. The stage is entered by a full-height steel door at the end of the maple wall, facing the Arts International offices. The front surface is comprised of two full-height panels that roll into various positions, depending on how the stage is being used.

The walls of the offices behind the stage are delineated by 1-foot-thick maple frames. These 8-foot by 8-foot maple frames create a dialogue with the steel boxes floating on the maple wall supporting the stage ceiling.

The plan suggests the many and varied events that will take place in the programmed areas. The large gallery has several uses: as a performance space, with the conference room used as a stage; as a gallery with the perimeter walls used for the display of art; as a gallery with the centre of the space used as a sculpture court; as a video display space with the perimeter walls and central space linked into video monitors; as a lecture hall with the conference room used as the stage; etc.

A 30-foot-long white silk curtain makes an edge so that it's possible to walk around the gallery without interrupting performances. The curtain adds a soft planar element to a project that is otherwise uncompromising in its strict adherence to hard geometries.

**view looking towards conference
room from entrance area**

opposite **view of office corridor, with conference room to left**

view looking into gallery from office area

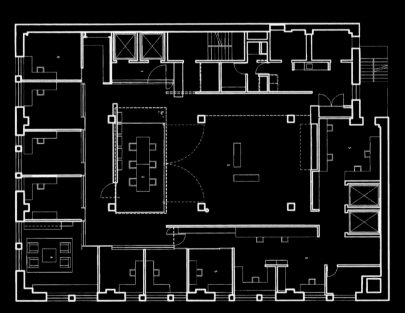

plan

looking towards entrance,
conference room to left

corridor in office area: framed space

looking towards conference
area/stage: framed space

opposite **detail of conference
room wall: steel boxes**

next pages **view from conference
room towards video wall: red
reflections to left, with blue
refracted light to right**

atmospheres

The atmosphere covers the earth in a blanket of repetitive and constantly changing experiences. It is the filter of the light that reaches us from the sun; it is not the source of light but it is suffused with light, colour and reflections. The atmosphere is filled, and we are constantly aware of the movement of clouds and water through it. We can experience this fullness in an aeroplane, flying through the layers of clouds and vapour across large expanses of space. An atmosphere is a medium; it conveys waves of sound, turbulence and magnetic deformation. In the 20th century, science has revealed the complexity of these fields of waves, deformed by the forces of heat, friction and magnetism. The sensation of an atmosphere is something that is all around us, inviting us to move freely over great distances, and bending and twisting us in its moments of intensity and turbulence. An atmosphere is never the same from moment to moment; it constantly changes over time.

The projects in this section are similar to atmospheres. They are light, spread out, and spatially indeterminate. They are light because of their transparency or the way they use light to cut spaces out of solid volumes. They spread repeating elements across an area, whether it is an interior, a city, or a landscape, filling it with minimal means in the same way a gas fills a bottle. The projects can be seen as indeterminate because the particular arrangements of the elements are a momentary order, evolving out of the particular circumstances of programme (Holley Loft), context (WaterLine) or topographical and site conditions (Ojai). These projects are intended to convey an atmospheric sensation.

Holley Loft creates a field of particles that are either solid blocks or transparent and moving planes. The blocks are essentially wood furniture (storage cabinets) and the planes are doors or windows, eliminating any conventional walls or divisions. The atmospheric sensation at the Holley Loft is of moving through a single space around solid particles.

In the case of the WaterLine project in Lower Manhattan, the strategy of dispersing similar elements is again used, but the repeating element is the opposite of a solid. A series of holes and voids acts as optical devices that convey light. These optical 'instruments' are dispersed across a large urban area, strategically intensifying urban relationships. The vertical dimension of towers and the sensation of occupying the sky in these voids capture the unique atmosphere of living in a city of skyscrapers. The optical void is the element that begins to open the material solidity of the city.

The Ojai Festival Shell attempts to capture the unseen complexity of the aural. By accepting the circumstantial arrangement of trees and the topography of a site, the acoustical space of the theatre bends and distorts itself around these points in space. The primary element of the architecture is the structural module, and, like sound waves in a finite space, they act as a stable datum in a turbulent field by maintaining their continuity from the stage openings back to the dressing rooms. The sensation here is one of moving through a continuous medium, conveying sound and light through semi-transparent materials. The sensation of atmosphere is both seen and heard, an immersed experience.

Thomas Hanrahan

opposite **windmills in the California desert**

Holley Loft

New York, New York

1996

**standing in bedroom looking out
towards glass and steel wall**

This project is an adaptation of an existing 4000-square-foot industrial loft space into a residence. The space is on the second floor of a loft building in lower Manhattan.

The design evolved from explorations of ambiguities between public and private by means of partial enclosures and transparent materials, and the character and use of the space.

The space centres around a music gallery. A glass and steel wall facing the gallery is a blank slate for musical notation and a reflective surface for sound. The gallery with its grand piano is the heart of the space, and an interior focus.

As the design developed, the space assumed a dispersed and open character. In the final design there are no solid internal walls. At any moment, from any position, the intention is to experience the full dimension of the loft, with elements of the programme distributed freely in the space. This yields a complex space of changing perspectives and points of view. Movable panels allow for the creation of smaller, more intimate spaces to accommodate guests in the area adjacent to the master bedroom.

A full-height glass and steel wall marks the major division of master bedroom and bath from the rest of the apartment. Curtains telescope in and out from two bays in the centre of the wall where sandblasted glass panels give privacy to the bath.

Opposite, a maple cabinet contains a curved steel and glass wall. This cabinet also marks a boundary between the music gallery and the kitchen and guest bath.

Full-height painted wood panels close down the rear of the apartment. Open, the panels float in the space; closed, they demarcate one room; closed further, two rooms.

The rear wall is a bookcase and storage cabinet. This linear planar element makes a loosely defined library.

opposite **pivot door looking towards
library; behind: flexible space**

plan

opposite **movable panels dividing
the space: flexible space**

collage massing study: flexible space

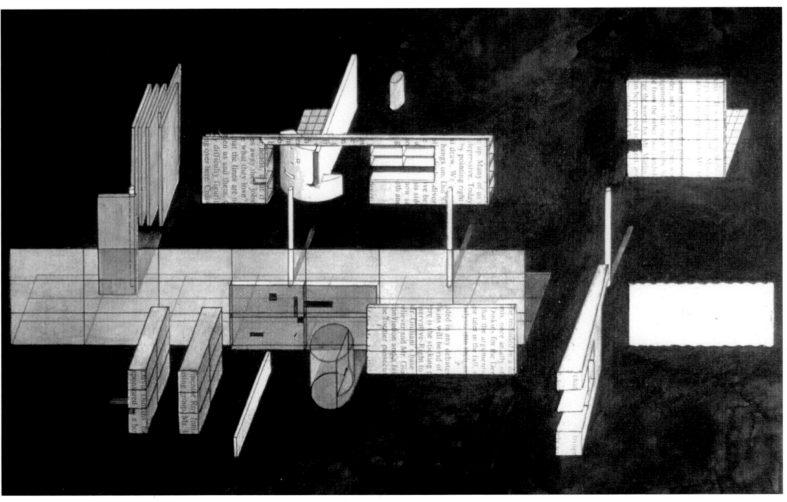

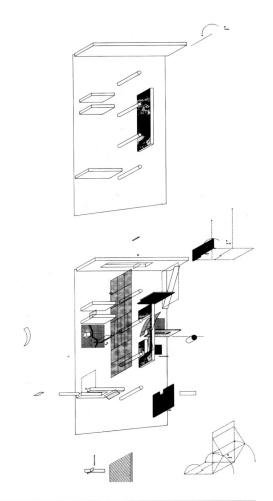

model

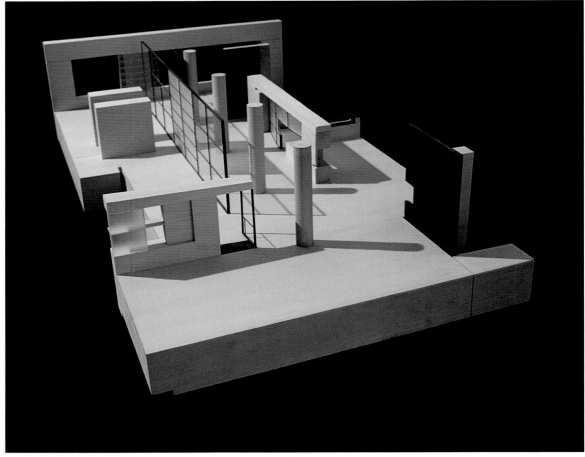

opposite **view of living area
from entrance**

opposite **free-standing steel wall adjacent to dining area**

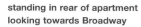

master bedroom

standing in rear of apartment looking towards Broadway

view from entrance looking towards
dining room

view looking from Broadway elevation towards rear
of apartment, steel and glass wall in foreground

Sagaponack House

Sagaponack, The Hamptons, Long Island, New York

2001

This design for a new house for the international development being planned in Sagaponack, New York, is conceived to emphasise transparency in its lower level. The house covers 3200 square feet, and is designed so that owners have the option of three bedrooms with an artist's studio, or four bedrooms including a separate suite for guests.

Transparency on the lower level of the house allows the surrounding Long Island landscape of grasses literally to flow through the ground floor. The lower-level enclosure is frameless glass, and the volume of the house at this level is defined mostly by the hovering mass of the second floor above.

The house is planned to be wood clapboard with glass and wood windows. The informality of the lifestyle in the Hamptons is emphasised in the design, which places a living room, entrance vestibule, kitchen and carport on three sides around a new deck that is planned as cedar. Guests can stay in a discretely separate wing that can also be used as an artist's studio, and this wing is entered by its own private stair adjacent to the carport.

perspective view
looking into courtyard

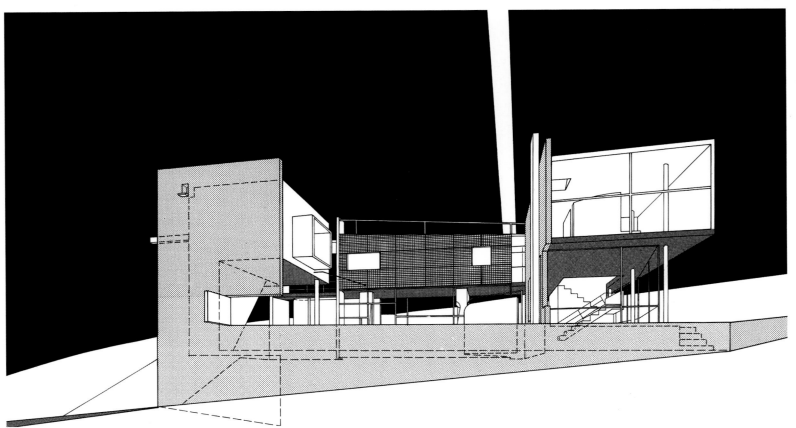

model view looking into courtyard

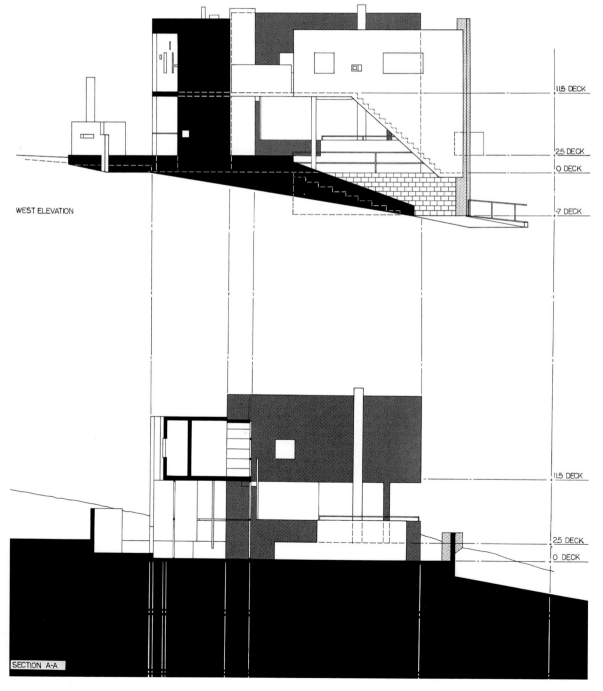

SECTION A-A

WEST ELEVATION

11.5 DECK

2.5 DECK

0 DECK

-7 DECK

11.5 DECK

2.5 DECK

0 DECK

west elevation and section A-A

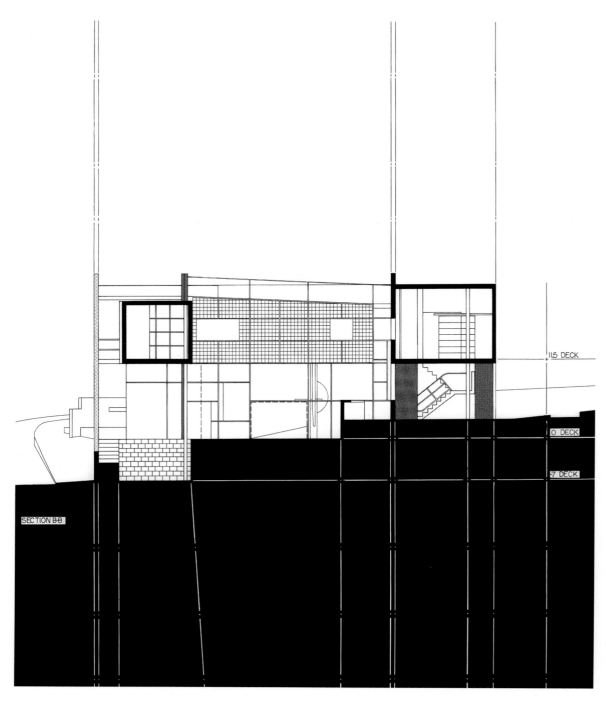

section B-B

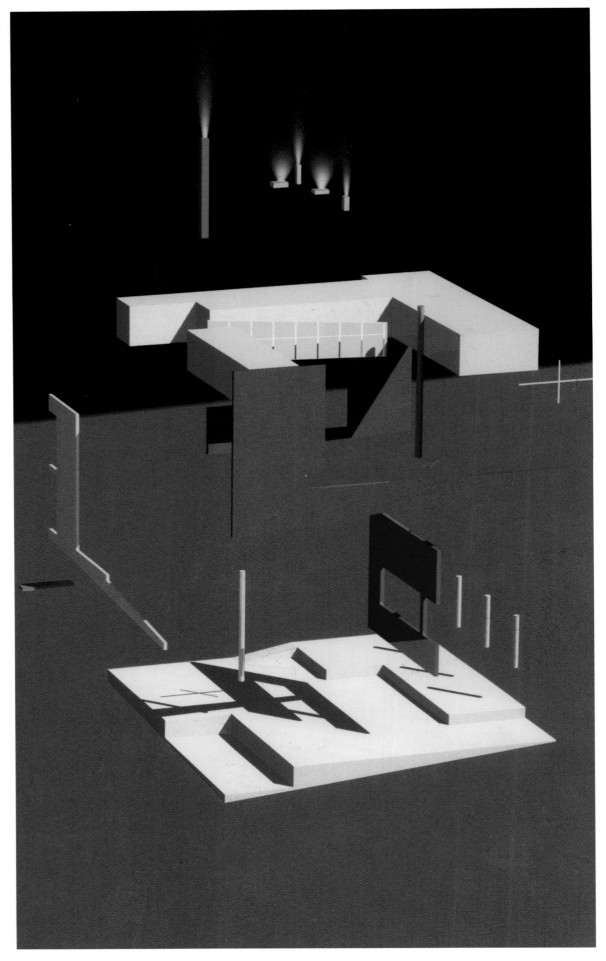

solid massing hovering above a
transparent base

second floor plan

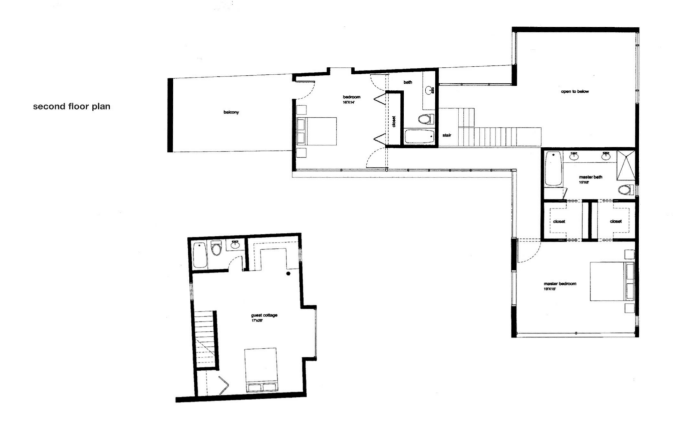

balcony

bedroom
16'X14'

bath

closet

stair

open to below

master bath
15'X8'

closet   closet

master bedroom
19'X15'

guest cottage
17'x28'

ground floor plan

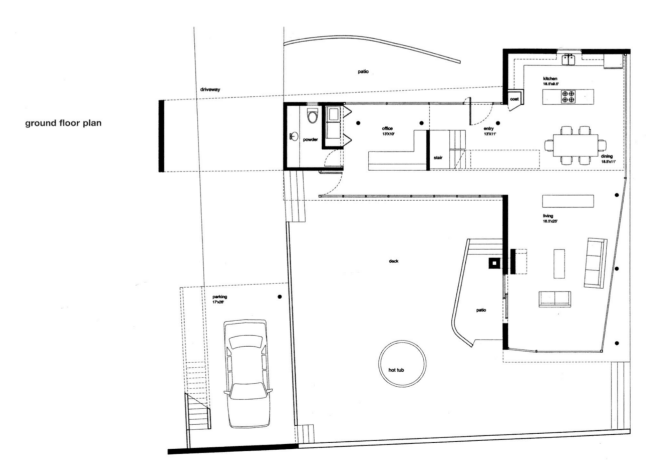

driveway

patio

kitchen
18.5'x8.9'

coat

powder

office
13'X10'

entry
13'X11'

dining
18.5'x11'

stair

living
18.5'x25'

deck

parking
17'x28'

patio

hot tub

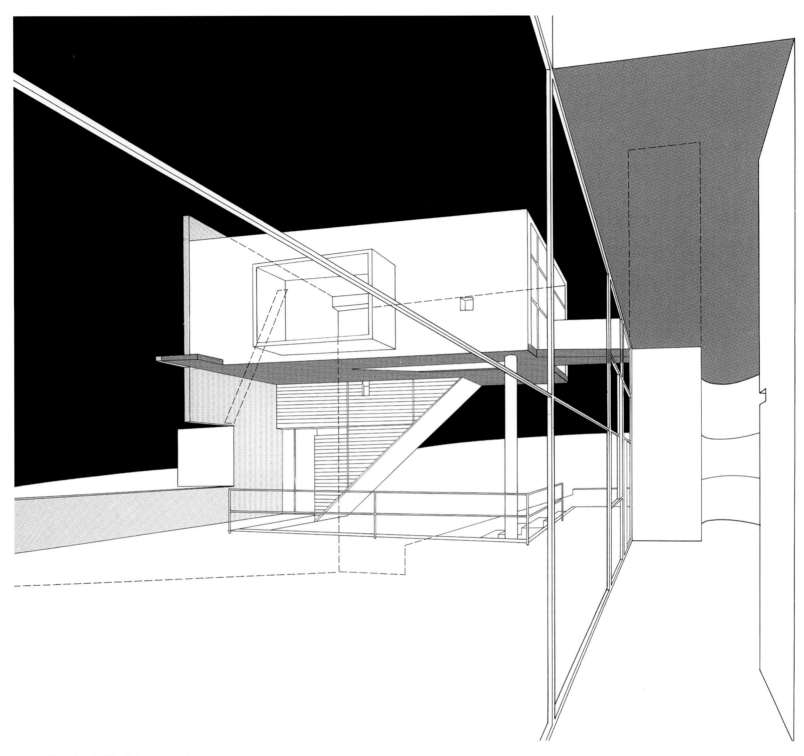

perspective view looking into courtyard

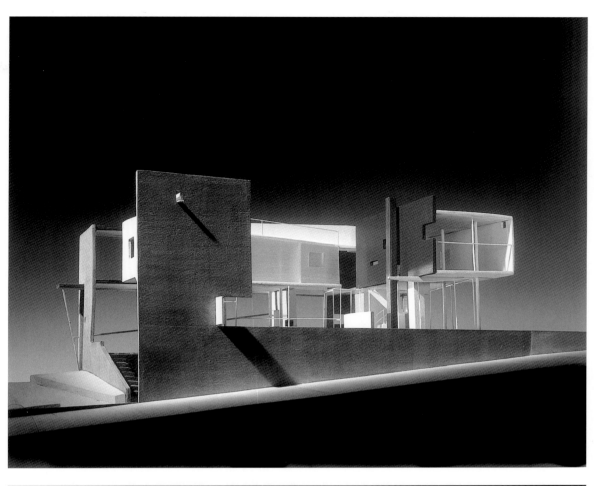

model view looking into courtyard

model: view looking through
transparent base

WaterLine

1992

WaterLine is a proposal for the Hudson River waterfront on the west side of Manhattan, from Battery Park to 59th Street. Throughout its early history New York was defined by its waterfront. Reading the American author Herman Melville, one glimpses a very different time, when the waterfront was the City's centre. In the City's more recent history the water's edge has become notable for its blight and neglect.

WaterLine is a proposal for clusters of public and private development at Manhattan's significant cross-streets: at 59th, 42nd, 34th, 14th and Canal Streets, along West Street facing the Hudson River. New public buildings where these streets meet the river are proposed to foster new development on the waterfront. A more detailed proposal about WaterLine was made at Canal Street.

A large open plaza marks the centre of the development at Canal Street. This plaza is bounded by a curved building that makes an edge towards the City, and a screen for outdoor films that marks an edge between the plaza and the river. The screen links the interior of the City to an evolving waterfront park. As a visual element this screen becomes an 'eye' to the City. A school for the performing arts occupies the top floors of the curved building marking the northeastern edge of the Canal Street Plaza. Performances by students can be projected onto the screen.

Information for monitoring the environment is collected from the skin of the southernmost tower of this block. The tower collects information about the air, light and noise levels in the City. It houses the former Department of Docks and Piers which is now an environmental and social monitoring agency. The tower has an assembly of air, light and water monitoring equipment on its southern face. The building's function is to monitor the environmental statistics of the City: the tower is the City's 'ear'. A figural element winds its way through the complex volumes of the City's 'ear', to appear as a disruption within the tower's west facade. This is a single-family residence for the City Statistician.

Three housing blocks to the north are a further part of this WaterLine proposal. The spatial typology of the housing creates an 'open' fabric within the density of New York. The WaterLine Plaza and its adjacent housing complex propose buildings that are hybrid both programmatically and formally. The buildings wrap themselves through and around blocks of space and create picturesque sequences linking the urban fabric to the water. This system of warped and skewed buildings slices through the dense fabric of Manhattan, forming a series of parks and public spaces in between. When these buildings cross the street grid, their facades are cut, with glass curtain wall inserted at moments of intersection.

Open space, new technologies, and the idea of living in the air suspended over water define a new urban edge at Canal Street. WaterLine is a formal strategy of warped and skewed space combined with new programming to propose a unique development in urban typologies. From West Houston to Canal Street pedestrians encounter a variety of semi-enclosed spaces. These transform from a triangular piazza at West Houston, to a tree-filled courtyard at King Street, to a water court that stretches from King Street to Vandam, to a new plaza linking Manhattan to the Hudson River and the harbour at Canal Street.

Changing spatial forms from north to south correspond to different natural settings: from arboretum, to artificial lake, to garden, to open ocean and harbour view. WaterLine explores possibilities for urban space, the skyscraper, new programmes for living and working, and the relationship between New York and its environment. It is this connection of city, landscape and environmental technologies that makes WaterLine a new departure in urban development.

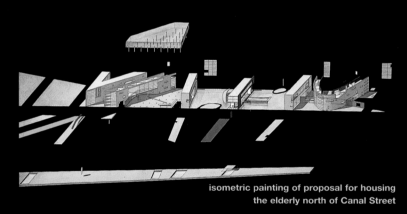

isometric painting of proposal for housing
the elderly north of Canal Street

plan: housing for
the elderly

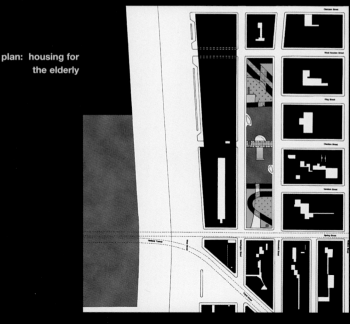

isometric massing study: Canal Street
municipal building

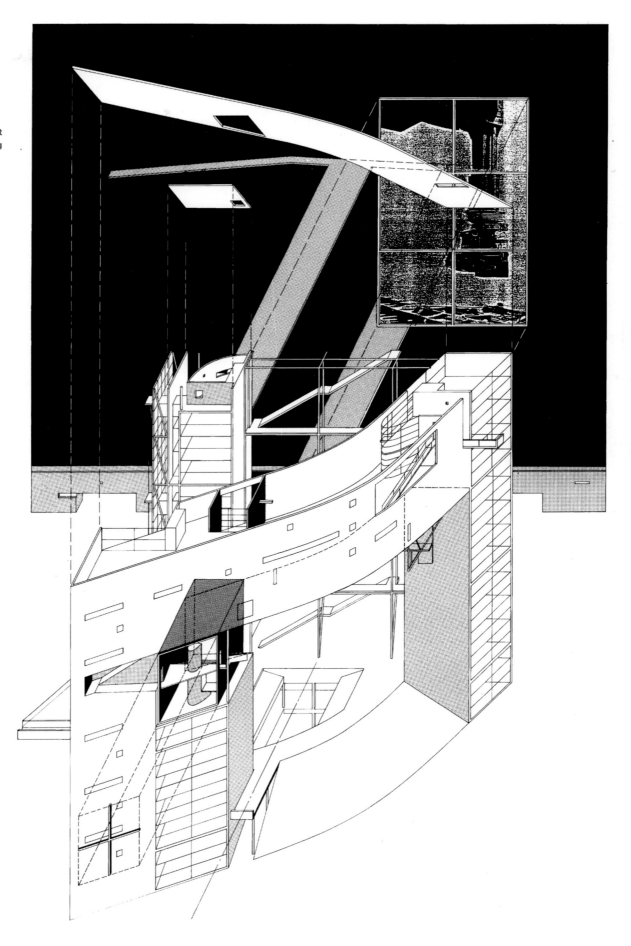

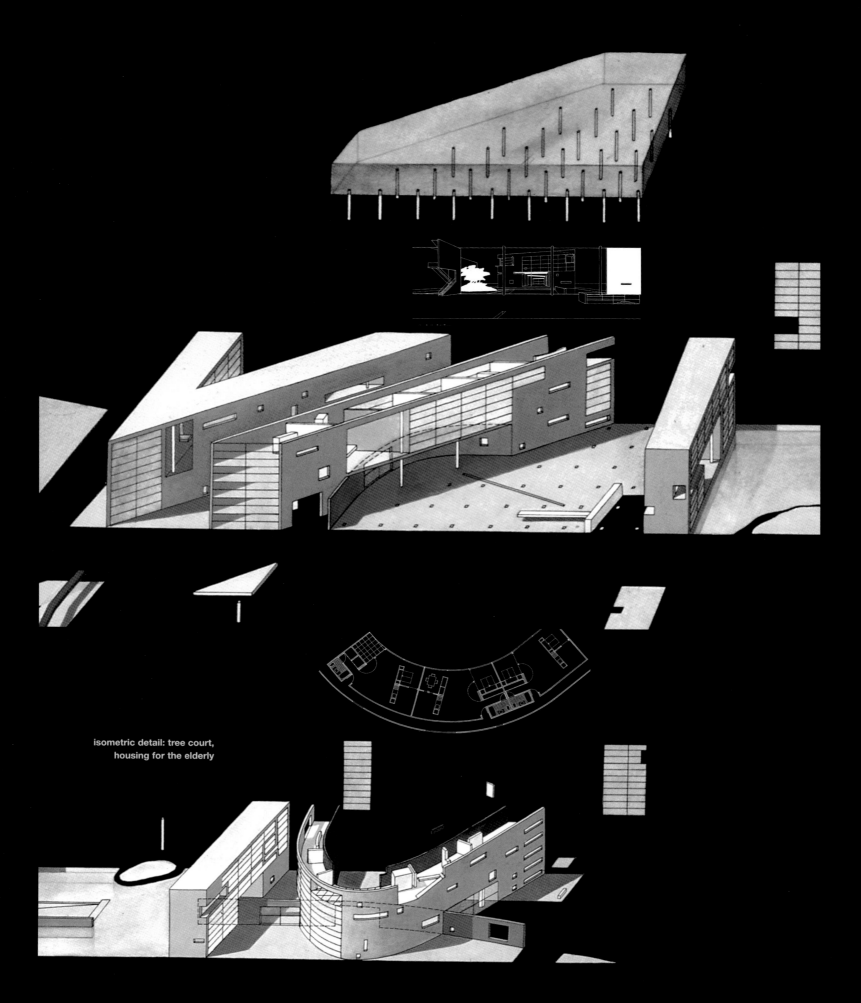

isometric detail: tree court,
housing for the elderly

view from Canal Street looking towards public stair
to new plaza within Canal Street municipal building

municipal building: bridging West Street

bridge over West Street with projection
screen connector between tower and
municipal building

'Particle Urbanism'

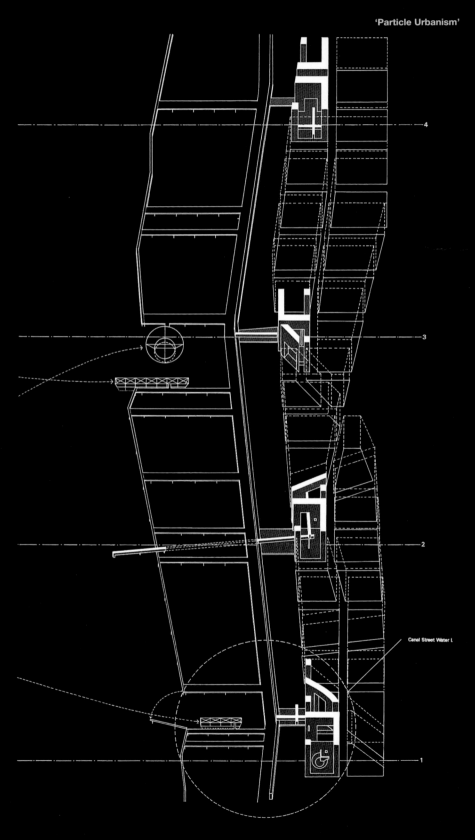

Canal Street Water L

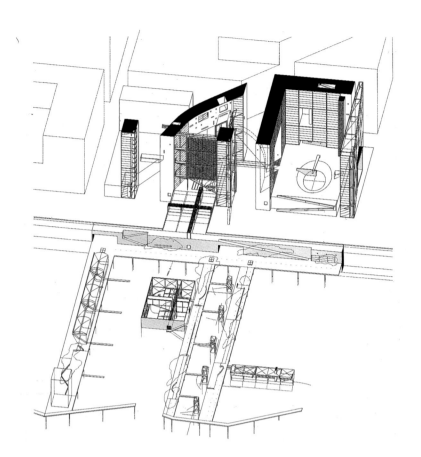

isometric detail of Canal Street complex: 'Particle Urbanism'

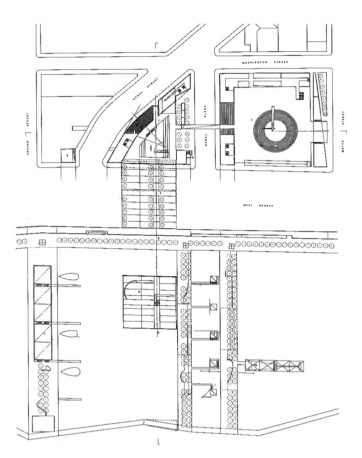

plan of Canal Street complex

Canal Street municipal building: section through entrance stair, public piazza, West Street piazza, and Holland Tunnel ventilation building

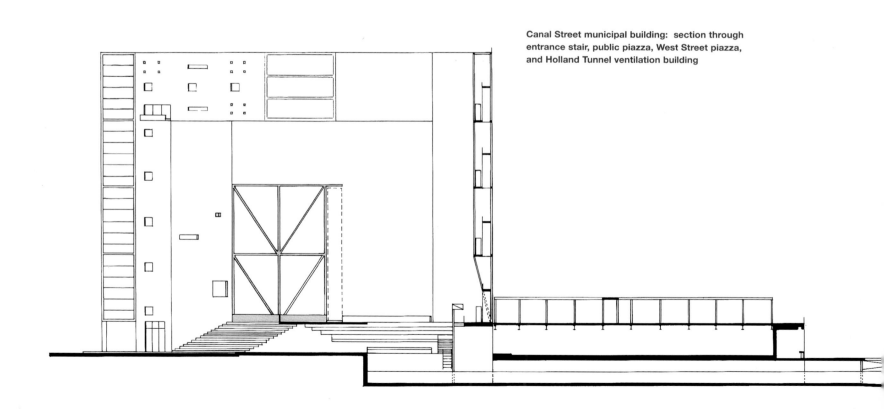

Canal Street performance wall section model

Canal Street theatre with Holland Tunnel below

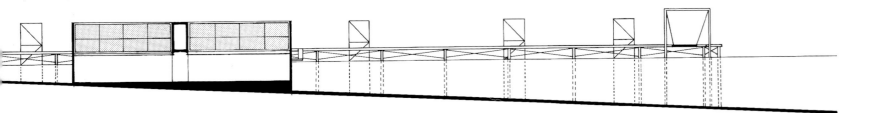

Listening Tower: skin as sensing
device

tower detail: the city's 'ear' (the
building that listens to the city)

section through water tunnel and screen

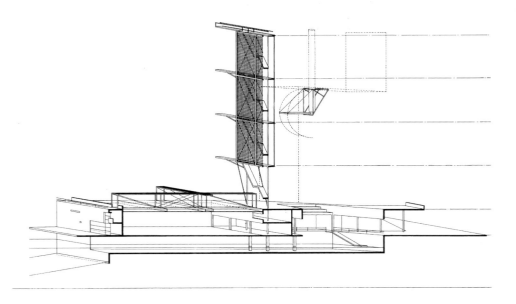

perspective view looking into
courtyard: performance space,
Holland Tunnel below

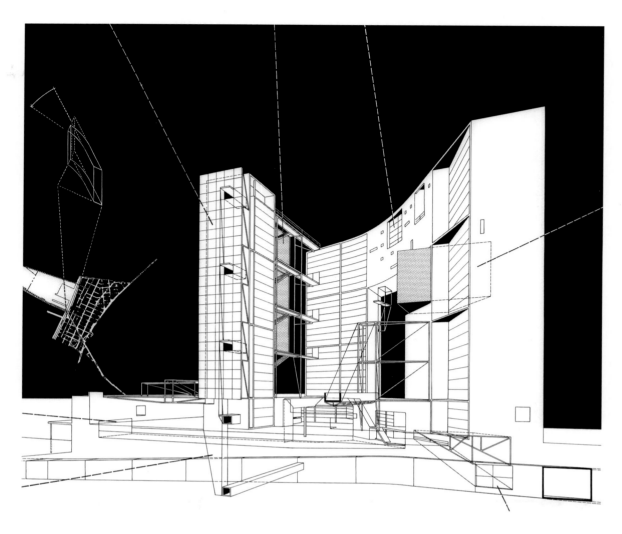

north–south section through Canal Street complex

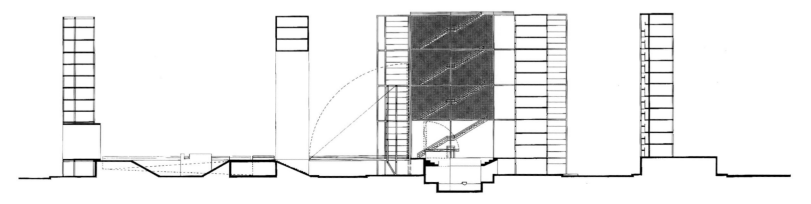

Ojai Festival Shell

Ojai, California

1999

The Ojai Festival Shell is conceived as 'sound made visible' – a reference to the statement of the Latin scholar Boethius that "music is number made audible". At Ojai a haptic 'sound field' makes space tangible as it unfolds through the mechanism of sound. Similarly to the way in which the composer John Cage made the Ryoanji garden in Kyoto tangible through sound, the space at Ojai is made visible through sound.

The Ojai Festival Shell is to be constructed as a hard acoustic inner shell wrapped by a translucent, glowing outer skin. The inner shell is an organic calcification of bone attached to a translucent skin that allows light to permeate it. Combining sound and light, the Ojai Shell is a celebration of the energy fields that make art possible.

At Ojai sound projects from the shell, creating a 'sound field'. The building becomes part of the landscape through sound. The 'sound field' is marked by discreet interventions: a bench, a piece of a wall, a boulder, a freestanding column. The traditional division between stage and backstage is blurred as the 'sound field' also extends into the backstage and courtyard. The continuous form of the building wraps around itself.

Libbey Park has been the summer home for the Los Angeles Philharmonic since 1966. An ancient arched sycamore tree in the heart of the Libbey Bowl stands as a sentinel to the days when the Chumash Indians would bend a young tree to mark a sacred spot. The Libbey Bowl sycamore, known as the 'Marriage Tree', is still used in rites of union and peace.

Since the Ojai Festivals began in 1947 they have amassed a heritage of world premieres from composers such as Stravinsky, Copland, Messiaen, Carter and Boulez. Ojai is also where famous conductors begin their careers and where new works by living composers are performed.

The green court in the shell developed because the City of Ojai is very protective of trees. In order to design a shell that is large enough to mix the sound properly and accommodate support spaces such as artist dressing rooms, a language was developed for the band shell as a 'building that wraps itself around trees'.

Musical sound and light determine the dimension of the seating area on the lawn: this is set by the distance that sound and waves travel. The outer skin of the shell is made of translucent glass panels that glow at night. Just as sound waves announce a musical performance, light emanating from the shell will draw patrons into the park for performances. An architectural choreography of sound and light was the objective for the new Ojai Festivals Music complex.

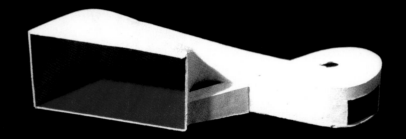

study model: Ojai shell as instrument for sound

plan sketch: Ojai performance shell

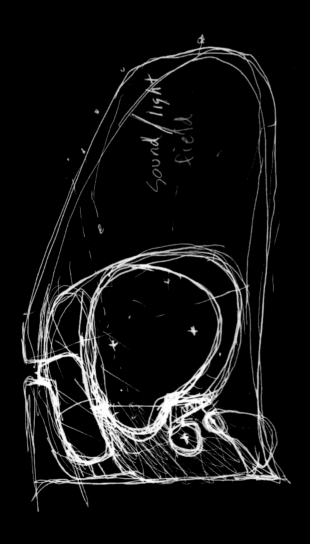

side elevation: looking towards sacred tree

rear elevation of building

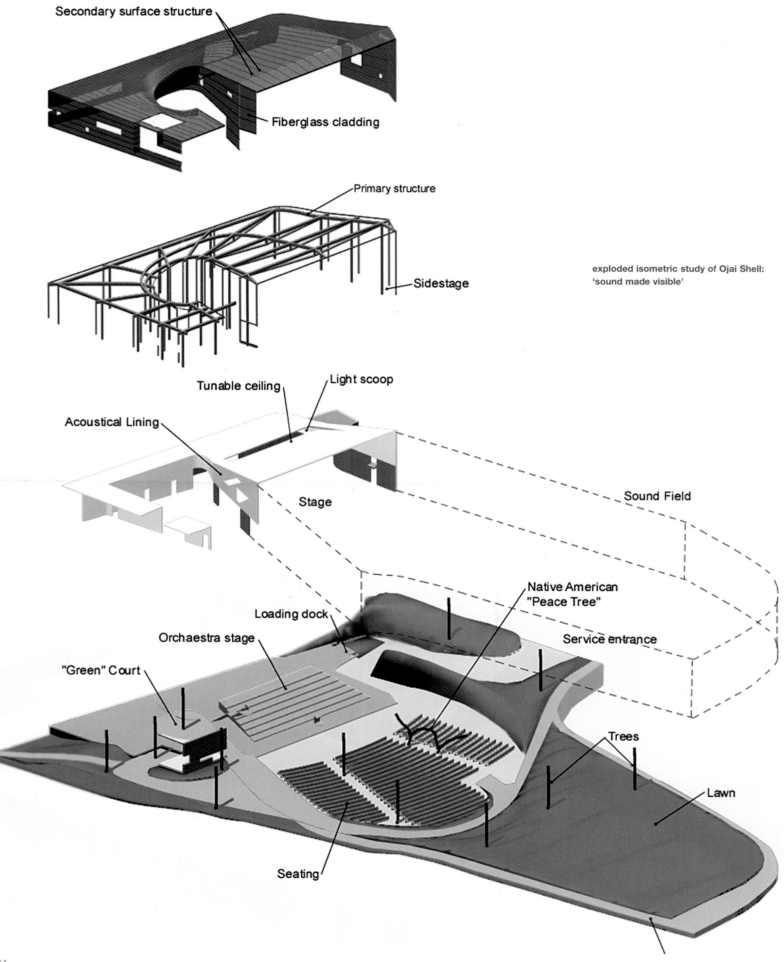

Secondary surface structure

Fiberglass cladding

Primary structure

Sidestage

exploded isometric study of Ojai Shell:
'sound made visible'

Tunable ceiling

Light scoop

Acoustical Lining

Stage

Sound Field

Native American
"Peace Tree"

Loading dock

Service entrance

Orchaestra stage

"Green" Court

Trees

Lawn

Seating

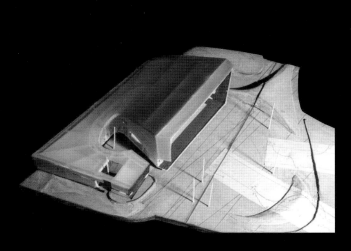

model view: visible sound

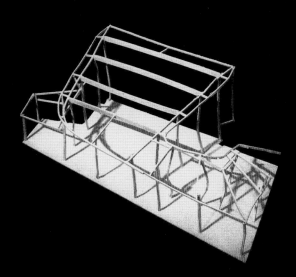

wire frame: shell structure

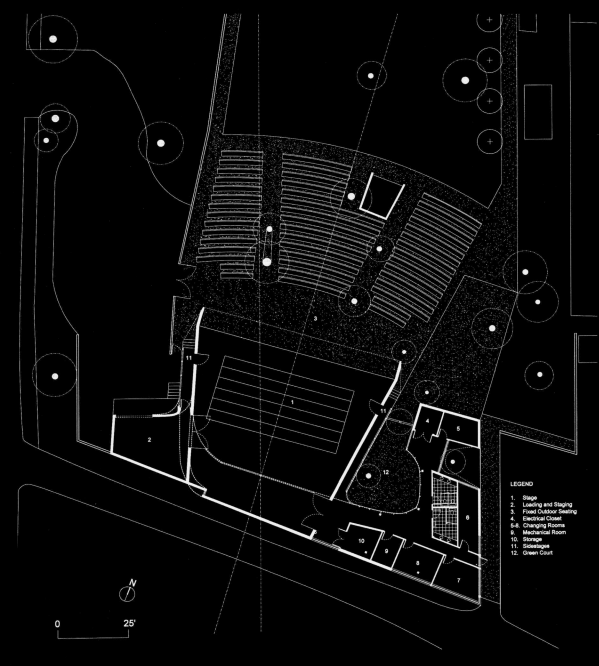

LEGEND

1. Stage
2. Loading and Staging
3. Fixed Outdoor Seating
4. Electrical Closet
5-8. Changing Rooms
9. Mechanical Room
10. Storage
11. Sidestages
12. Green Court

N

0   25'

ground floor level plan

night view: Ojai Libbey Bowl

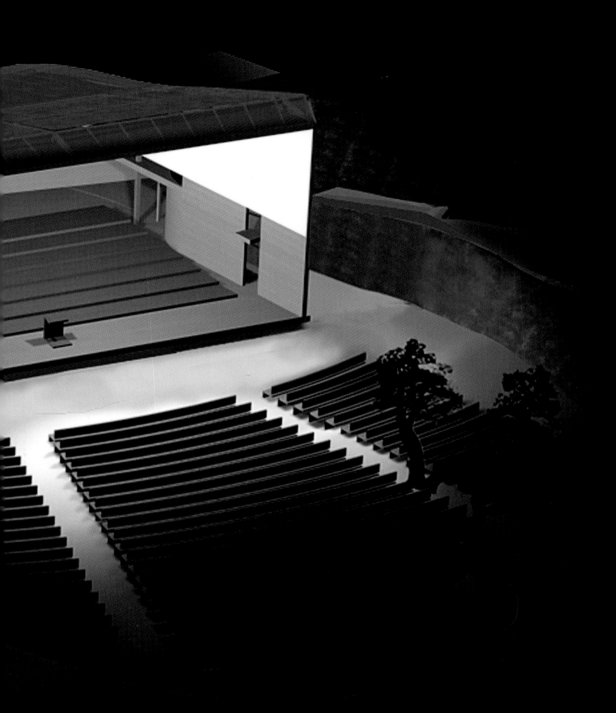

view standing in green room

opposite **night view looking towards stage**

green court looking towards
green room

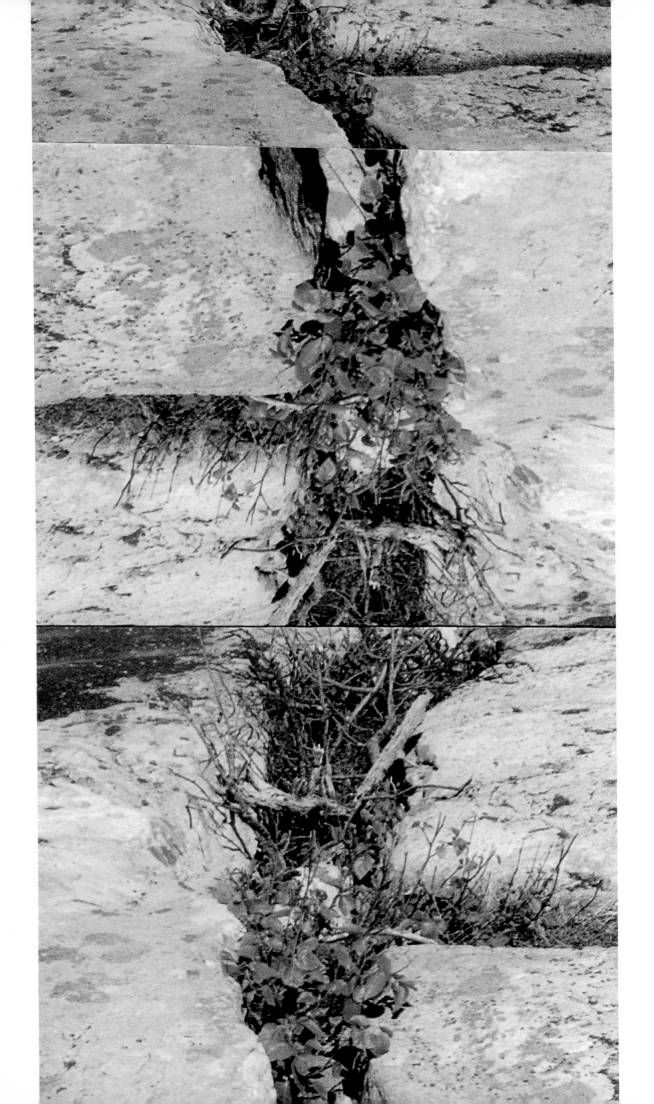

ground

Ground is a word that often describes something that is stable and under our feet, for example when our 'feet are planted firmly on the ground' or we are 'well grounded'. In reality the ground is not stable, but a dynamic, layered crust of materials in motion. The projects in this section reflect this actual sense of ground, as they are textured, opaque and complex in form. These projects are conceived as extractions from the earth, as vessels or volumes shaped by solid material. Most of these projects reduce the programme of the building into singular volumes, but they are not reductive in character. The surfaces that surround these spaces resemble the complexity of the surface of the ground itself. These surfaces are textured and layered, like the woven vegetation that covers the earth (Hunts Point Performance Center or the Museum of Women proposal). The projects also can be seen as an eruption of the ground surface like a sand dune rising up from a plain (WaveLine), or as a vessel of space shaped by forces found in the earth (Alves House).

When the ground is viewed from above, satellite photographs reveal systems and organisations of bewildering complexity. Ridges ripple unexpectedly into sharp peaks, or just as suddenly drop into flat deltas where the force of water scours the surface of the earth. Zooming closer, the rise and fall of the ground compresses and relaxes, creating perspectival depth and shaped spaces. Examined closely in section, the precise character of the ground increases in complexity as well. The organic processes of exchange between plants, animals and inorganic materials suggest that the ground is a layered organism from treetop to ocean bottom. The ground is not a single plane, but layers of creased and woven surfaces.

The four projects that follow capture all these characteristics. The Hunts Point Performance Center and the Museum of Women explore the layered and filtering quality of the ground by projecting various section profiles onto a single roof or wall plane. The Alves House draws more directly from its context by using the geometries of the ridge and adjacent streambed in the design of a tapered volume that stretches from north to south. The interior of this house is virtually one space where all these projected geometries are visible simultaneously. The WaveLine project is a surface that ripples upwards from a flat, urban setting. The scored metal cladding follows these contours from one end of the project to the other. This project is again a single space, transformed by the spirit of spaces that are given to us by accidents of nature.

Thomas Hanrahan

opposite **seamed landscape**

Hunts Point Performance Center

Bronx, New York, New York

2001

Hunts Point Performance Center comprises a performance space, gallery, and art education centre. The site is Julio Carballo Fields, a park in the Bronx. The building was designed as a 'virtual forest' to give back the land that it occupies, virtually, as forest.

The sense of a virtual forest inside the building was created through the manipulation of light and structure. A landscaped area in front of the building includes a grid of trees that continues inside the centre through structure. The light falling through tree branches is captured through natural light penetrated into the building through skylights. A series of virtual landscape elements – park benches, kiosks and skylights – imples the presence of a forest or garden.

The ground floor houses an entrance, art gallery, a theatre/multi-purpose room, and dance and rehearsal rooms. These are inwardly focused rooms.

The second floor, which is reached by ascending the 'waterfall' stair, is outwardly focused with walls that are mostly glass. A gallery makes a path that rims the upper level of the performance space below, and looks out to framed views of the park.

The roof is a giant arch that opens to the park. The arch frames the tops of the surrounding trees, and delineates a swath of space within, a 'virtual forest'. The roof is punctuated by skylights that are yellow and green.

Hunts Pont Performance Center is a proposal about bringing the green of the forest into the heart of the city.

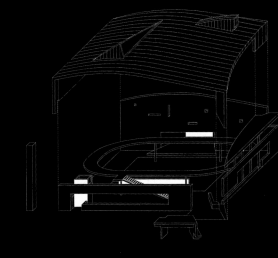

isometric study: performance space

window detail: 'virtual forest'

east elevation: building entrance

north elevation

window detail above entrance

ground level plan

upper level plan

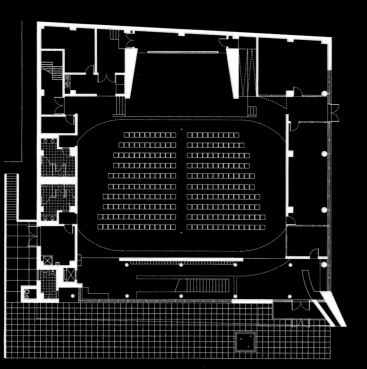

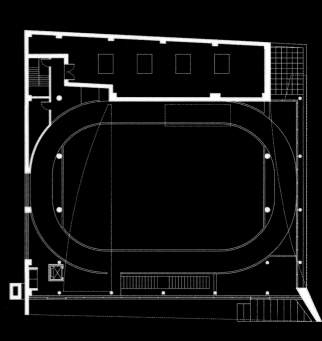

view from window towards park

section diagrams

section diagrams

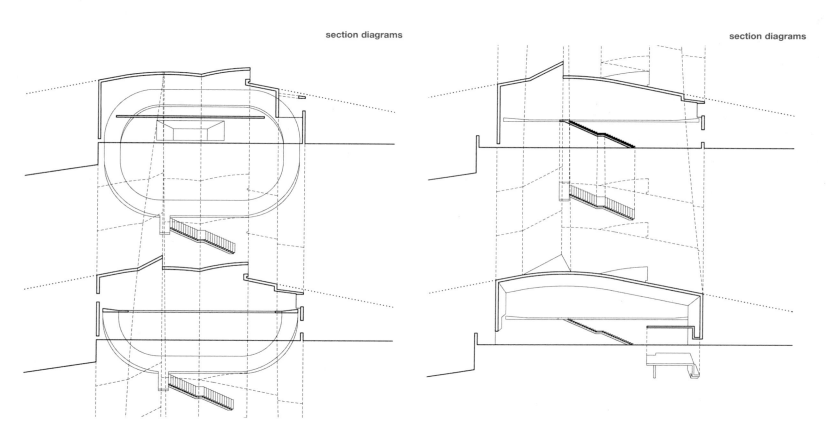

east elevation of model: stair detail

east elevation of model

opposite **stair to upper level**

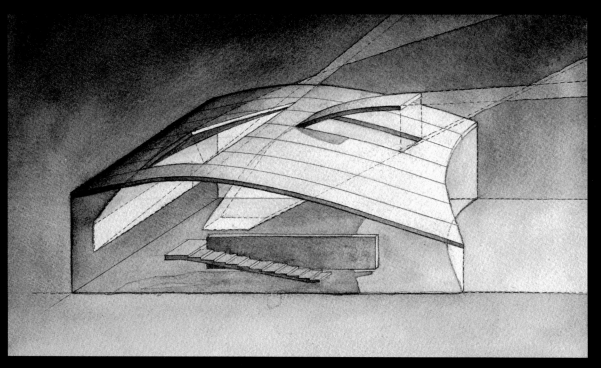

projected light and roof study

model detail of roof openings

opposite view of seating area
below, from upper level

next pages east elevation

The Museum of Women

Battery Park City, New York, New York

1999

The Museum of Women is a building that tells a story through its physical rendering on a site. It is an inclusive building that makes space for many colours and textures within its rich weave. The museum is made from woven fabric that creates a place for extended conversations between women, about women, and for women. Although it is based in Manhattan, through the Web the museum will connect women around the globe.

The basic design principle of the site for the museum, Battery Park City, is to create a seamless urban fabric. The museum, however, needs a clear identity. It is important that every aspect of the museum embodies its mission.

The building's text will include the role of women in history, their role today, and their place in the future. Part of this fabric is a 'timeline'. The timeline speaks about women's role in various cultures: as it is, as it was, and as it will be.

Along with an investigation into the life of Susan B Anthony and Elizabeth Cady Stanton, and other women active in the fight for women's rights, the preparations for the project included collecting 'testimonials' from women throughout the United States. These testimonials addressed what it means to be a woman, each writer's experience of the women's movement, and how being a woman or experiencing the women's rights movement affected the writers' lives.

The testimonials were gathered from many sources to form a rich base for research and preparation for the design of the museum. These gathered testimonial texts were bound into the design of the building.

The skin of the building tells a story about the history of women in the United States. It also uses weaving and layering to make an environmentally sensitive enclosure.

The museum is a transparent building covered in a 'woven fabric'. This fabric is a series of sunshades and rain-catches that make the building an ecologically sensitive ecosystem. The skin will be an important part of that ecosystem, keeping the internal temperatures and humidity levels controlled with a minimum use of fossil fuels. This layered and woven skin is environmentally sensitive and uses sustainable technologies.

The woven nature of the building takes on many forms. The weave is literal and subtle, with woven areas of light and dark, and woven circulation patterns underlining a narrative text and creating a 'web' to hold the conversations that the building fosters. The building will be a centre of convergence for this fabric, with threads reaching into the landscape of Battery Park, and Web connections relating the building and the stories it generates to a worldwide audience.

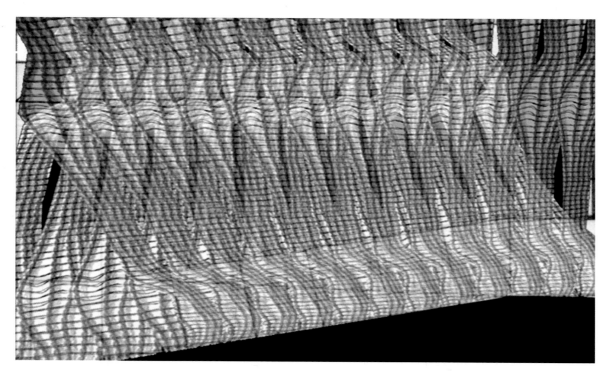

elevation study: elevation as 'fabric'

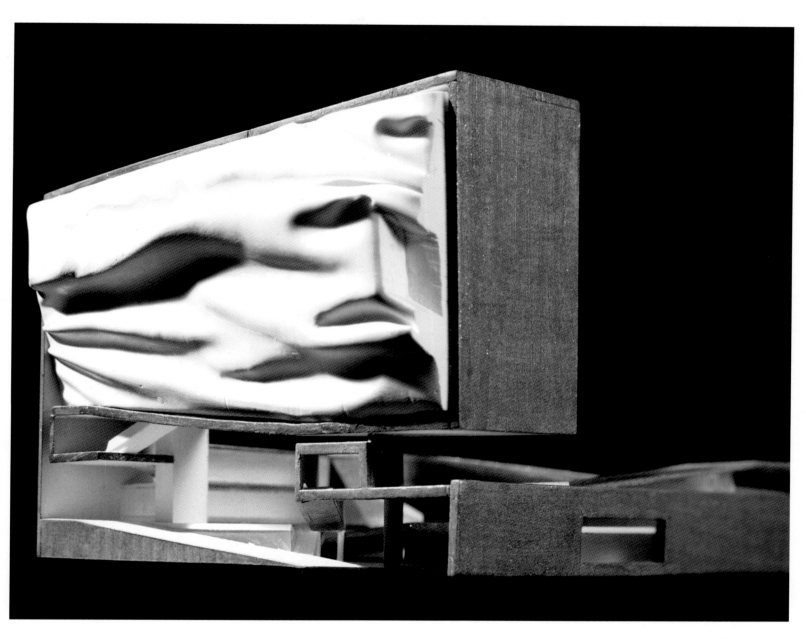

model and view: a woven fabric as building elevation

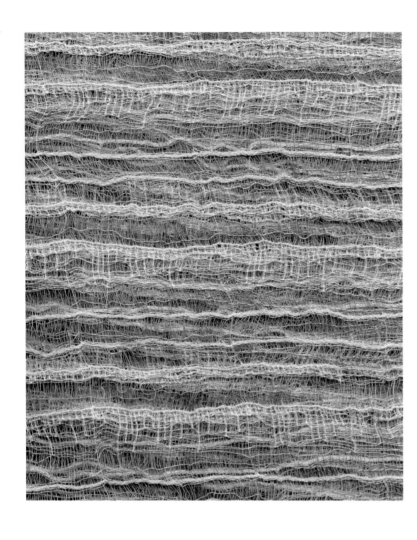

a woven fabric: stories from women
around the world

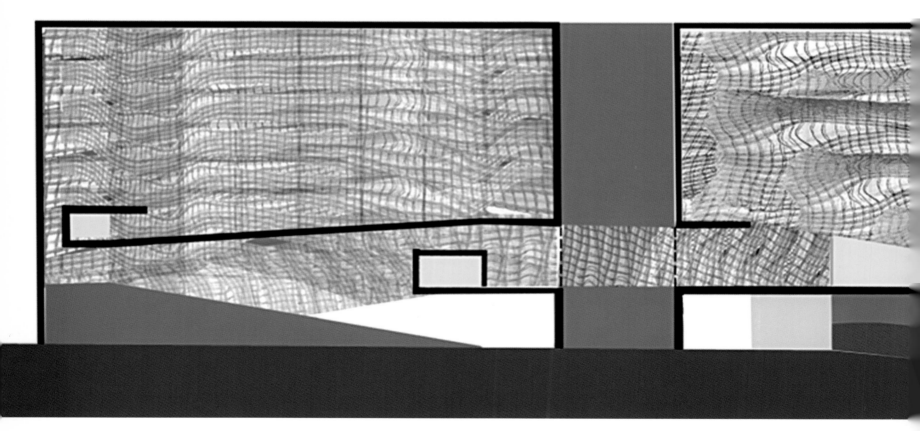

context model

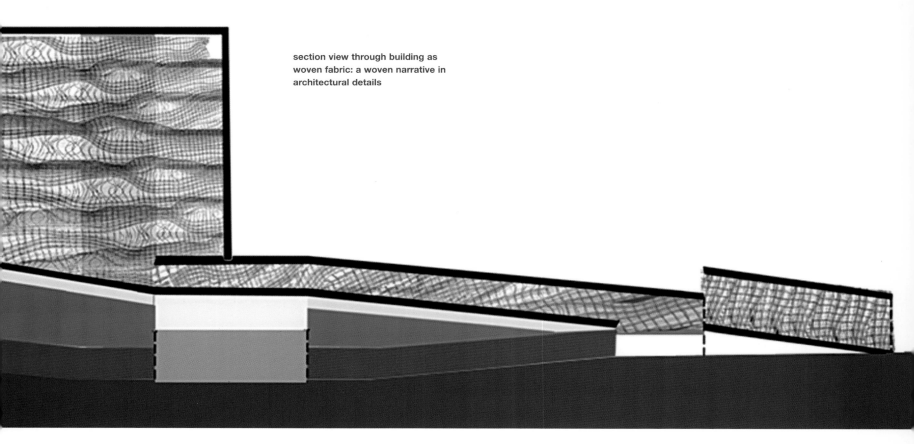

section view through building as
woven fabric: a woven narrative in
architectural details

Alves House

Northampton, Massachusetts

1998

This house in central Massachusetts was designed as a vessel shaped by different kinds of light. The area of the site where the house was constructed is a shelf of flat land on a steep slope that faces south and east. Given the small buildable area available and the size of the programme, the house was designed as a single space: a modulated volume excavated by light.

The design began with letters from the client describing a desire for a house with the primal quality of a single room, almost cave-like in its character, while capturing as much light as possible. There is a tradition in this part of the United States of building wood structures that simulate the interiors of wood ships. Along the New England coast carpenters who constructed ships also built homes and churches using details borrowed from their ship-building experiences.

In *Moby Dick* Herman Melville describes a small church where a chaplain pulls a stair up to his pulpit as if departing on a boat prior to giving his sermon. Light filters into the room from above, and sailors are seated in the nave beyond. From these details abstract ideas about a single vessel were transformed into a house.

The house in its final form is an elongated volume constructed of ship-lapped cedar. Entrance is from a stone terrace through a deep, sculpted wall. The stone extends into the house to create a ground floor related to the earth.

A steel stair drops down to this floor from a second-floor deck that leads to the master bedroom. Covering this floating deck and the first floor is the outer shell of the house.

The second-floor deck extends through the master bedroom and creates an elevated outdoor seating area to the east. This affords a view of the mountains to the south. This extension of the house creates a dining room sheathed in copper below.

The house fulfilled the aspirations of the client as a place to contemplate the cycles of nature. It does this through a series of details that allow them to take journeys of the mind from within a vessel of light.

watercolor massing study: a folded plane as house

opposite **view looking at south elevation**

interior detail: bridges of steel and stone walls

living room view: towards dining room bridge

section

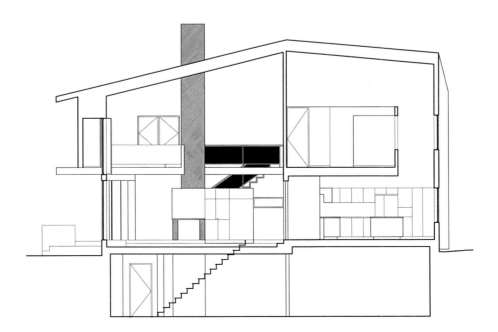

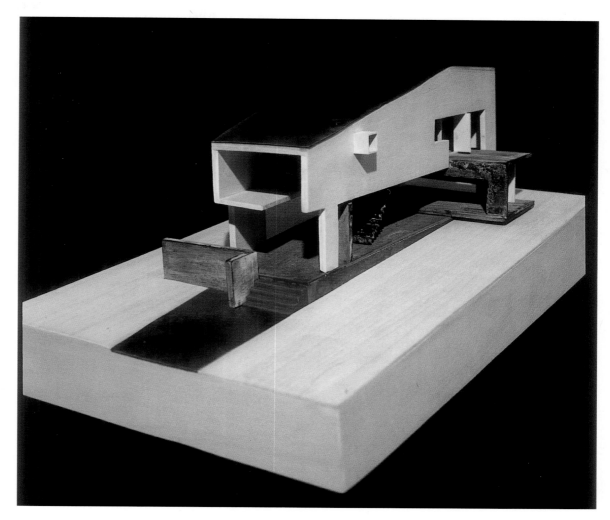

model view: house as folded tube

isometric view of wood shell over masonry base   site plan   next pages view of south elevation

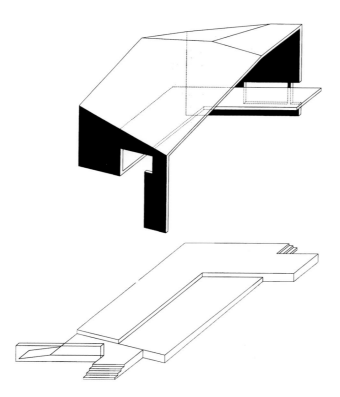

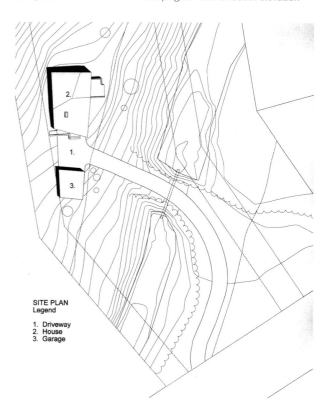

SITE PLAN
Legend

1. Driveway
2. House
3. Garage

WaveLine – Latimer Gardens Community Center

Queens, New York, New York

1997–2002

Desert wind moves across the landscape, picking up particles, depositing debris beyond an initial ripple, creating ever-new ripples. One ripple leads to more ripples. WaveLine was an attempt to create an insertion into an existing landscape in Queens, New York, which would have a similarly dynamic effect on its surroundings.

WaveLine is located on 137th Street in Flushing, Queens on a site that includes four high-rise housing blocks owned and managed by the New York City Housing Authority. Hanrahan + Meyers were hired to design a 4500-square-foot multipurpose theatre and gym adjacent to an existing community centre. Through the form of its roof, WaveLine refers to ideas of flow and flux in physics.

The roof, the principal design feature of WaveLine, is a bent plane running from east to west and resting on columns. It will be visible from the housing blocks surrounding it and was designed as a sculptural shape with standing-seam stainless-steel cladding. The roof folds down to create both the east and west elevations. As a continuation of the movement suggested by the roof, a reflecting pool to the east cuts into the ground plane, extending the wave movement, and creating a second 'ripple'.

'Wave-line', a term originating in ship building, refers to the optimum outline for the hull of a vessel to facilitate movement through the waves, as recommended by naval architects. The term is also applied in physics to the path of a wave of sound or light.

WaveLine's roof was designed as a wave structure which creates a sense of flow within a spatially constricted site. This formal gesture constructed in stainless steel creates a topography of ripples and wave formations. The ripples or waves of this new landscape fold into themselves the possibility of new public spaces, a place for theatre, and areas of recreation.

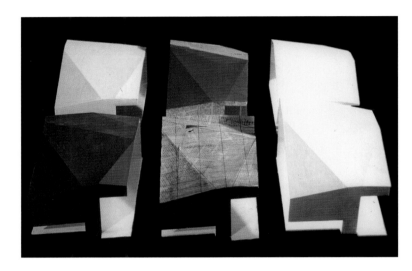

studies of roof shapes: waveline

opposite **perspective wire frame**

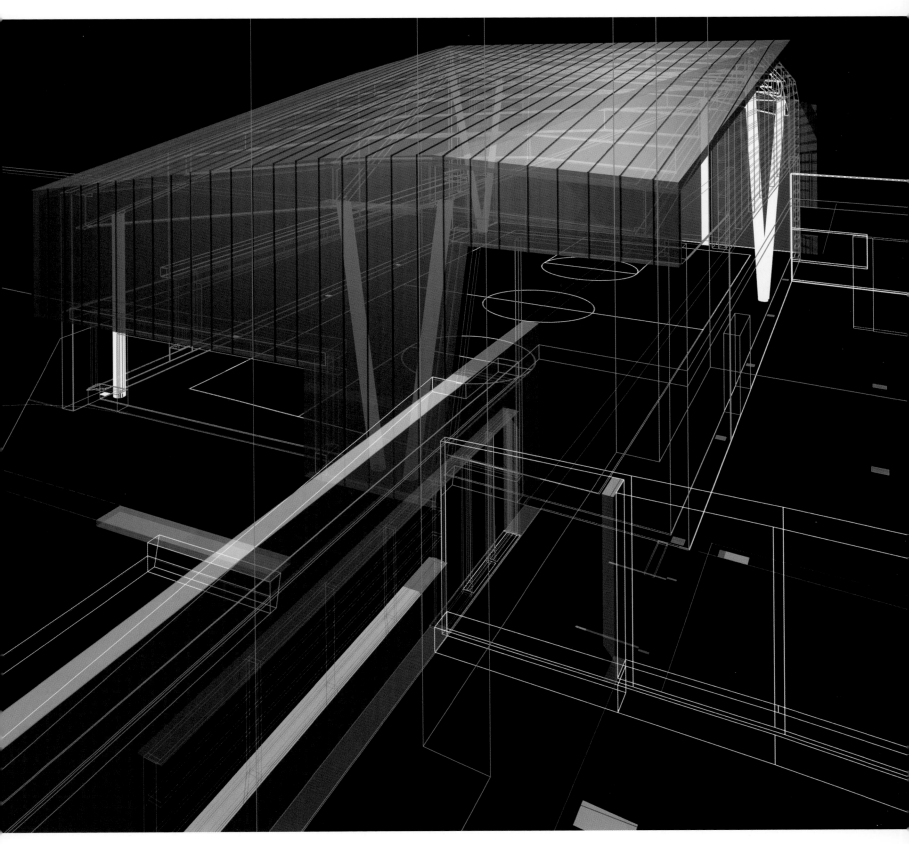

plan

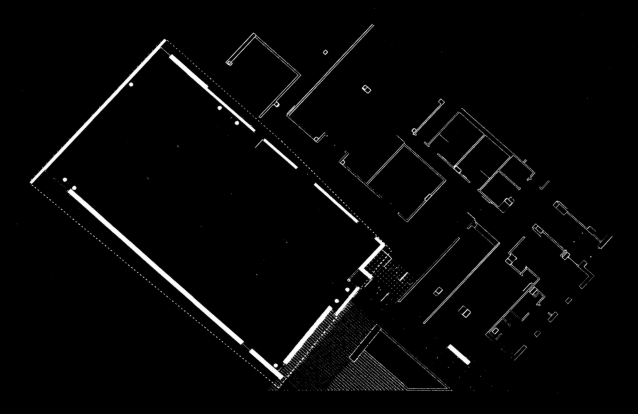

section

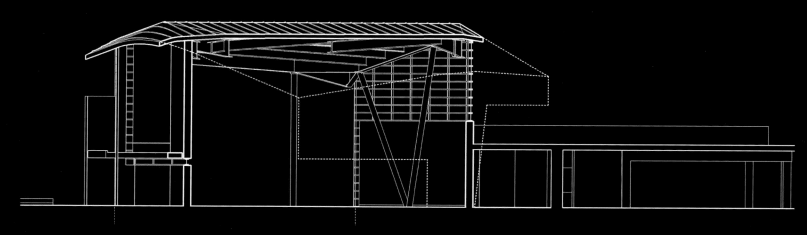

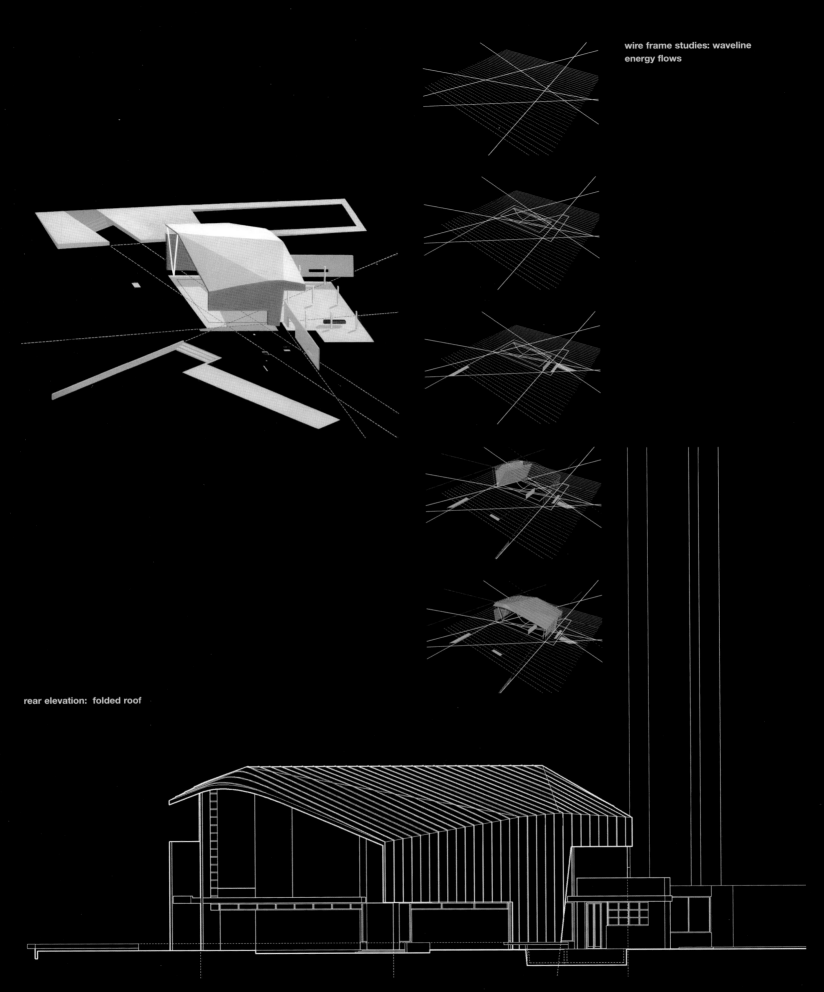

wire frame studies: waveline
energy flows

rear elevation: folded roof

perspective view inside waveline building

model view: waveline

model view: building section

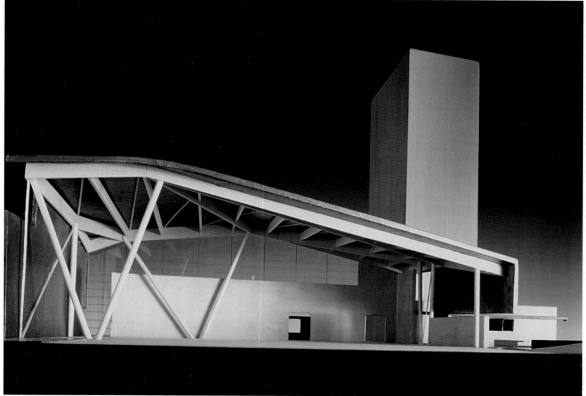

Hanrahan + Meyers

Victoria Meyers and **Thomas Hanrahan** have practised in Manhattan and Los Angeles since 1985. Their work includes projects of many scales and diverse programmes, from large urban proposals to individual residences. In 1993 they received the commission for the AIA New York Chapter Headquarters after submitting a winning design in a competition. Their work was featured at the Museum of Modern Art in 1999 and includes galleries, performance spaces and residences for private clients. Their current projects include an arts centre in Brooklyn, New York, a performance centre in the Bronx, New York, a performance pavilion for the New York City Housing Authority in Queens, New York, and private houses and lofts. The public sector projects bring a unique focus on arts spaces and arts education. These projects focus on large performance spaces and galleries for art as well as classrooms. Hanrahan + Meyers are architects for a new outdoor Performance Pavilion for the Los Angeles Philharmonic in Ojai, California, and have worked successfully with various not-for-profit arts groups, including Arts International and the Academy of American Poets. Recently Hanrahan + Meyers were commissioned to design a house for the Sagaponack Project, an international housing development in East Hampton, New York. In 2001 Hanrahan + Meyers opened a new office in Los Angeles, California.

Victoria Meyers was born in Abilene, Texas. She received a MArch from Harvard's Graduate School of Design and an AB in Art History/Civil Engineering from Lafayette College in Pennsylvania. Her work in architecture reflects a broadly based cross-disciplinary background. Her studies of light from natural and artificial sources are being catalogued in a book she is writing under contract with John Wiley & Sons Ltd, London. These studies have led to unique solutions for galleries and performance spaces. Victoria's apprenticeship in the office of the British architect Richard Rogers exposed her to an environmentally complex approach to building design, emphasising a unique approach to mechanical, structural and other energy-related systems. Victoria sees the crafting of materials and the study of colour and light as an important aspect of her design aesthetic. In addition to her practice Victoria also teaches architecture at Columbia University's Graduate School of Architecture, New York. She has gallery representation at Pierogi Gallery in Brooklyn, New York.

Thomas Hanrahan was born in Chicago, Illinois. He attended the University of Illinois at Urbana-Champaign where he received his BSArch. He received his MArch from Harvard's Graduate School of Design. Thomas also studied in Versailles, France under a scholarship from the University of Illinois, and travelled through central and northern Europe investigating modern European design under a Wheelwright Fellowship from Harvard University. These experiences have been decisive in formulating his interests in an experimental design method reflecting modern life and culture and in the crafting of materials. Thomas also brings experience in the planning of large-scale projects, first with Skidmore, Owings and Merrill, Architects, in Chicago, and most recently in private practice in New York as Hanrahan + Meyers' projects have increased in scope and complexity. Thomas Hanrahan has taught at Columbia, Harvard and Yale. He is currently Dean of the Pratt Institute School of Architecture, New York.